"Yesterday, the greatest question was decided which ever was debated in America, and a greater perhaps never was nor will be decided among men. A resolution was passed without one dissenting colony, 'that these United Colonies are, and of right ought to be, free and independent States.'"

JOHN ADAMS IN A LETTER TO ABIGAIL ADAMS

[JULY 3, 1776]

"That all men are by nature equally free and independent, and have certain inherent rights, of which, when they enter into a state of society, they cannot by any compact deprive or divest their posterity; namely the enjoyment of life and liberty, with the means of acquiring and possessing property, and pursuing and obtaining happiness and saftey."

GEORGE MASON, VIRGINA BILL OF RIGHTS

[JUNE 12, 1776], ARTICLE I

"They [the Americans] are the hope of this world. They become its model."

FROM THE LETTER OF ANNE ROBERT JACQUES TURGOT,

BARON DE L'AULNE TO DR. RICHARD PRICE

[MARCH 22, 1778]

THE DECLARATION OF INDEPENDENCE

and

THE CONSTITUTION OF THE UNITED STATES

Introduction by Pauline Maier

BANTAM CLASSIC

THE DECLARATION OF INDEPENDENCE and
THE CONSTITUTION OF THE UNITED STATES
A Bantam Book

PUBLISHING HISTORY
Bantam Classic edition published July 1998
Bantam reissue / May 2008

Published by
Bantam Dell
A Division of Random House, Inc.
New York, New York

ISBN 978-0-553-21482-6

Printed in the United States of America
Published simultaneously in Canada

www.bantamdell.com

OPM   40   39   38

CONTENTS

INTRODUCTION

THE AMERICAN TRIUMVIRATE:
THE DECLARATION OF INDEPENDENCE,
THE CONSTITUTION, AND THE BILL OF RIGHTS

AT THE "shrine" in the National Archives, just off the Mall in Washington, D.C., three parchment documents are on display. The most visible, enclosed in a heavy brass frame, standing like a tabernacle, high above the others, is the Declaration of Independence. Below it, on the surface of an "altar," lie the Constitution and the federal Bill of Rights. Today the three documents seem parts of a whole; they are the "founding documents" of the United States, the Americans' "charters of freedom." Their texts have become "political scriptures," in a phrase James Madison once used,[1] that is, statements of belief and practice written during the American Revolution to which generation after generation of Americans has returned for guidance and direction. Over time, they came to define the Americans as a people.

The three documents were first created to perform distinct, complementary functions. The Declaration of Independence (1776) was a revolutionary manifesto that proclaimed and justified the end of British rule over America; the Bill of Rights (1789–91) stated the basic rights of the American people, and the Constitution (1787–88) created a new federal government that would, hopefully, secure those rights. Americans learned to revere documents such as these from their English ancestors, who themselves had long honored written texts such as the Magna Charta (1215), a version of which is also on display at the Archives.

One such English "constitutional" document, the Declaration of Rights of 1688–89, provided a direct precedent for all three of the documents on display at the Archives. Its opening section officially brought to an end the reign of James II, who had, it said, endeavored "to Subvert and Extirpate the Protestant Religion, and the Laws and Liberties of this Kingdom" by a series of acts that it listed, much as the American Declaration of Independence listed the ways in which George III had attempted to establish "an absolute tyranny over these states." The second part of the English Declaration of Rights stated and "declared" the English people's "Ancient Rights and Liberties," as did the "declarations" or "bills of rights" that Americans wrote and attached to many state constitutions adopted between 1776 and 1780 and, later, to the federal Constitution. Finally, the English Declaration of Rights offered the British throne to James II's daughter, Mary, and her husband, William, Prince of Orange, on the expectation that they would better protect and preserve their subjects' "Religion, Rights, and Liberties."[2] In 1776 the Americans decided that the preservation of their liberty was incompatible with monarchy and hereditary rule. As a result, they established "republics," governments in which all authority came directly or indirectly from popular choice, and whose powers and institutional structures were described in written constitutions. Those constitutions were far more elaborate than the final provisions of the English Declaration of Rights, but, like those provisions, they established a new government, or "regime," that seemed more likely to preserve the people's rights and freedom.

The affection with which Americans regard the three "founding documents" of the United States has not been constant over time. In the 1790s, when Madison spoke of America's "political scriptures," he referred only to "constitutional charters,"[3] a category that included the Constitution and the Bill of Rights. The Declaration of Independence—now, as its prominence at the Archives suggests, probably the most beloved of the triumvirate—did not yet belong in the category. Moreover, the federal Bill of Rights took roughly a century and a half to exert the influence that made it a powerful national icon by the late twentieth century. The functions of the Declaration of Independence and Bill of Rights also changed, and in ways that, with the Declaration in particular, have served to obscure its original function. That helps explain why so many Americans, even some in high office, persistently confuse one of the founding documents with another. It also explains why understanding those documents requires not just a careful look at their origins, but a sense of how they changed, and why, over the next two centuries.

I. THE DECLARATION OF INDEPENDENCE

Independence was something most colonists wanted to avoid. Not even the outbreak of war at Lexington and Concord, Massachusetts, on April 19, 1775, ended the Americans' desire to remain under the British Crown.

Delegates to the Second Continental Congress, which
convened at Philadelphia on May 10, 1775, worked, as
their constituents insisted, for reconciliation with the
mother country and ardently denied charges that the
Americans wanted to found a "new empire" until January
1776, when, suddenly, with the arrival of still more news
that demonstrated the king's hostility toward America,
the denials ceased. But even then many delegates hoped
that royal peace commissioners would soon arrive and
end the crisis.[4]

The first copies of Thomas Paine's *Common Sense* appeared on January 9, 1776, then spread like wildfire
through the country. There was no going back, the pam-
phlet argued; American freedom could never be secure
under the British Crown. The time had come to correct
the "errors" in Britain's constitution and to found new
governments free of kings and hereditary rule, governments in which all officials owed their power to popular
choice. Soon not only congressional delegates, but the
American people were discussing whether the time had
come to found a separate American nation.

By the spring, towns, counties, and states began pass-
ing resolutions, or "instructions," to their elected representatives that told them to work for independence, and
frequently explained why. Sometimes the men who composed those early "declarations of independence" used
Paine's words, but seldom if ever did they repeat his central argument. In one case after another they founded
their conclusion not on the flaws in Britain's form of government, but on the way the king had treated Americans
over the previous year. They cited George III's refusal
even to answer the dutiful, loyal petition for peace the
Congress had sent him in July 1775; his approval of the

Prohibitory Act of December 1775, which made both colonial ships and ports vulnerable to attack by the Royal Navy as if they were owned by open enemies, thereby putting the Americans "outside his protection"; his making war on his American subjects, burning American towns, including Charlestown, Massachusetts, Falmouth, Maine, and Norfolk, Virginia; his enlisting both slaves and Indians against the colonists, and, finally, in the spring of 1776, contracting with German princes for "mercenary" soldiers to help reestablish his authority in North America. Now a crisis was at hand: the colonists would be destroyed unless they got help from some non-British ally, which they could not do unless they bade Great Britain "the last adieu." Then, as the freeholders of Buckingham County, Virginia, put it, "some foreign power may, for their own interest, lend us an assisting hand."[5] The decision for independence was born, in short, not of desire but of desperation.

Finally, on June 7, 1776, Richard Henry Lee, a delegate from Virginia acting on instructions from the convention, or extralegal assembly, that ruled his state, asked Congress to approve a set of resolutions. The first said

> That these United Colonies are, and of right ought to be, free and independent States, that they are absolved from all allegiance to the British Crown, and that all political connection between them and the State of Great Britain is, and ought to be, totally dissolved.[6]

The delegates discussed Lee's motion on Saturday, June 8, and again on Monday the tenth. The debates, as we know from notes taken by a thirty-three-year-old

Virginia delegate named Thomas Jefferson, were heated. Both sides admitted that independence had become inevitable, but they disagreed on the wisdom of adopting it immediately. Opponents argued that negotiations with France should begin first and, moreover, that the people were not yet ready for independence, and that the Congress had always wisely avoided taking so major a step until "the voice of the people drove us into it." Finally, the delegates decided to postpone the decision until July, which would give states that precluded their delegations from voting for independence an opportunity to change those instructions.

In the meantime, to prevent further loss of time once a decision was made, on June 11 Congress appointed a committee to draft a declaration that could be issued if Congress adopted independence. The committee had five members: Jefferson, who was a poor speaker and so seldom took part in congressional debates, but had a great gift for writing public documents; John Adams of Massachusetts, perhaps Congress's most outspoken and persistent advocate of independence; Robert R. Livingston, who had argued for delay in the debates of June and whose home state, New York, was especially hesitant to leave the Empire; the judicious Roger Sherman of Connecticut, and Pennsylvania's Benjamin Franklin, one of the oldest and most distinguished delegates, but a man so afflicted with gout that he attended few if any of the drafting committee's meetings.

The committee, John Adams recalled, had "several meetings, in which were proposed the Articles of which the Declaration were to consist, and minutes made of them."[7] That is, it discussed how the Declaration should be organized, and probably also what its various parts, or "articles," should say, then committed its conclusions to paper as "minutes," or instructions, for its draftsman. Adams's recollections were recorded long after the event, but they make sense: it's difficult to imagine the drafting committee appointing a draftsman without first discussing what he was supposed to do. Then the committee appointed Jefferson to realize its ideas on paper.

Adams also remembered that Jefferson produced a draft in a day or two, which is possible. Jefferson could write quickly, and he was working under severe time constraints. Like other members of Congress, he had to attend regular sessions of Congress throughout the day from Monday through Saturday, and probably did so because military affairs were approaching a crisis in both Canada and New York, requiring the Congress's attention. He also had other committee assignments to juggle while he worked on the Declaration, one of which required that he write two long reports—both of which were submitted to Congress in his handwriting—related to the Americans' disastrous invasion of Canada.

Like other writers forced to meet a tight deadline, Jefferson worked from two older texts (although he didn't remember that in the 1820s, when Americans began asking questions about the drafting). Within the previous few weeks he had written a preamble for the new, revolutionary constitution of Virginia that was, for all practical purposes, Virginia's declaration of independence. Jefferson still had an early draft of that preamble in his papers. He dug it out, then rearranged the charges it levied against George III and inserted others, some of which were based on events that occurred primarily in other states. He also eliminated the preamble's opening "Whereas" clause, which said George III had attempted to establish "a detestable & insupportable tyranny."[8] Jefferson had based that clause upon the opening passage of the English Declaration of Rights, but now he had a better idea. He opened the Declaration of Independence with two paragraphs that are today the most familiar and admired parts of the document.

"When in the course of human events," the words that open the Declaration, convey a sense of epic significance. The first paragraph then announced the document's purpose: to "declare the causes" of America's separation from Britain from "a decent respect to the opinions of mankind"[9]—which implied that mankind was watching and so added to the sense that the Americans' decision to "assume a separate and equal station" among the "powers of the earth" was indeed a historic event.

The next paragraph started with a long sentence that began, "We hold these truths to be sacred and undeniable," until someone, perhaps Franklin, substituted "self-evident" for its last three words. That sentence restated several basic political principles widely shared by Americans of the time: that all men were created equal; that they had, as Jefferson put it, "inherent and unalienable rights"; that to protect those rights men created governments, whose powers came "from the consent of the governed," and that whenever any government became "destructive of these ends," it was the "right of the people to alter or to abolish it, & to institute new government" in a way that seemed "most likely to effect their safety & happiness." The final, culminating assertion was the climax and the point of the sentence; indeed, the sentence was constructed according to a known eighteenth-century rhetorical method by which one phrase was piled on another, but their point became clear only at the end.[10]

It made sense to assert the right of revolution so dramatically in the Declaration of Independence: after all, it was the right Americans were exercising in 1776, and the Declaration was designed to demonstrate that they did so with justice.

The people's right to alter or abolish and replace standing governments was not to be exercised, the paragraph went on, "for light & transient causes." But "when a long train of abuse & usurpations" revealed a settled design to subject them to absolute rule, it was not just the people's right but also their duty to "throw off such government, & to provide new guards for their future security." The Declaration then asserted that George III was guilty of protracted "injuries and usurpations" that revealed his intention to establish an "absolute tyranny" over the American states. The document proceeded to demonstrate the truth of that assertion by stating a series of "facts"—the charges against the king. Both the Virginia preamble and the English Declaration of Rights began their charges against the king with the word "by" ("by keeping among us, in times of peace standing Armies and Ships of War," for example).[11] Most charges in the Declaration of Independence begin instead "he has." Jefferson's draft said, for instance, "he has kept among us, in times of peace, standing armies and ships of war, without the consent of our legislatures." By opening the Declaration of Independence with something other than a short "Whereas" clause and by rephrasing the charges against George III, Jefferson distinguished his draft Declaration from its English ancestor of 1688–89. In that way he effected a certain literary independence like the political independence that the Declaration announced.

In composing the second paragraph of the Declaration, Jefferson probably also drew upon a draft Declaration of Rights for Virginia written by a respected Virginia planter and public servant named George Mason. That document appeared in the *Pennsylvania Gazette* on June 12, 1776, perhaps the same day Congress's drafting committee first met somewhere in Philadelphia. Did the committee ask Jefferson to adopt language like Mason's? Did he do it on his own initiative? We'll probably never know, since whatever "minutes" the committee wrote have long since disappeared. Textual evidence indicates, however, that Jefferson began with Mason's sprawling statement of what eighteenth-century Americans often called "revolution principles," which he compressed into a far briefer statement of the same ideas. The Mason draft said, for example, that "all men are born equally free and independent," which Jefferson altered to say "all men are created equal and independent." Then he crossed out "and independent." Mason said that men "have certain inherent natural rights, of which they cannot, by any compact, deprive or divest their posterity; among which are the enjoyment of life and liberty, with the means of acquiring and possessing property, and pursuing and obtaining happiness and safety." Jefferson wrote instead that men had "rights inherent & unalienable," which he changed to "inherent & unalienable rights," using "unalienable" to replace the long phrase that began "which they cannot . . ." He also abbreviated Mason's lengthy statement of men's inherent rights into first "the preservation of life, & liberty, & the pursuit of happiness," then simply "life, liberty, and the pursuit of happiness."[12] Jefferson had to be concise: what Mason had said in three substantial clauses of his draft Declaration of Rights he needed to state in a single sentence that explained and asserted the right of revolution. Then he could show that the Americans' exercise of that right was justified. Jefferson was, after all, not writing a "declaration" or bill of rights; he was explaining the end of the old regime, not, like Mason, laying down the principles that would bind its successor.

Jefferson's use of Mason's text (which became something of an "instant classic" in revolutionary America) was perfectly in keeping with the ethical standards of his time. The eighteenth century put little value on originality in the sense of creating something entirely new. Instead, young men were taught to study the great writings of the past and, where appropriate, adapt them for their purposes. The highest praise went to writers or orators whose written or spoken adaptations exceeded the models of excellence upon which they were based.[13] The sentence that Jefferson created from Mason's text was not just beautifully crafted, but played a critical role in the logic of the Declaration. After listing the "long train of abuse and usurpations" George III had supposedly committed, the document concluded that the king was indeed a "tyrant," as the second paragraph had asserted.

Then, after a long section castigating the British people for refusing "to disavow these usurpations," the draft Declaration drew its final conclusion—that the Americans were justified in exercising their right of revolution by throwing out their old government and founding another more likely to serve their safety and happiness. "We therefore"—that is, for all the reasons previously stated—"the Representatives of the United States of America . . . in the name and by authority of the good people of these states," the last paragraph said ". . . assert and declare these colonies to be free and independent states..."

The text Jefferson first showed to other committee members underwent extensive revision before being submitted to Congress on June 28. Late in life Jefferson remembered showing the text to Adams and Franklin, whose suggestions he particularly valued, and said the committee finally approved the draft with no further alterations.[14] In fact, the committee was far more active than he recalled. A note Jefferson sent to Franklin with the draft Declaration in June 1776 says that the committee had scrutinized the text and returned it to him "to change a particular sentiment or two," and that once he received Franklin's suggestions—hopefully by the next morning—he planned to lay it before the committee again.[15] Obviously, some of the editorial adjustments marked on the "original rough draft" of the Declaration (now one of the Library of Congress's most treasured documents) were made by Jefferson on orders from the drafting committee, which asked him to make revisions that were more than minor verbal adjustments, and planned to go over the text once again before submitting it to Congress. He probably forgot that when, almost fifty years later, he examined the "original rough draft," which he still possessed, he noticed that all the changes were in his handwriting except for a few inserted by Adams and Franklin, and assumed that those he wrote were made on his initiative. That would have been an honest mistake, but a mistake nonetheless.

After receiving and reading the draft Declaration of Independence, Congress promptly tabled it. Then, on

July 2, after approving Lee's resolution with the consent of all the states except New York—which added its endorsement more than two weeks later—the delegates took up the draft Declaration. The context was forbidding: final news that the American invasion of Canada had ended in pitiful disarray arrived in early July just as British ships began appearing off New York, where Britain was assembling one of the greatest military and naval forces ever seen in North America to put down, once and for all, the colonists' "rebellion." Nonetheless, the delegates spent the better part of two days editing the draft Declaration.

And it needed a good editing. The delegates left most of the opening two paragraphs untouched: those Jefferson had already worked over carefully. They did, however, change Jefferson's "inherent & unalienable rights" to "certain unalienable rights." They also pruned back some of Jefferson's extreme language—saying, for example, that the colonies were forced to "alter" rather than "expunge" their former system of government, since the Americans wanted to keep some parts of the old system, such as trial by jury and elected legislatures. Congress also accused the king of "repeated" rather than "unremitting" injuries. That was more accurate: sometimes months, even years, had gone by with nothing much happening.[16]

Jefferson's charges against the king also needed editing. His list—which included some twenty-one accusations, plus nine "pretended acts of legislation" mentioned under the thirteenth of those charges—was much longer than those in other, similar documents. Most state and local "declarations of independence," for example, mentioned only five or six well-known events. Moreover, many of the abuses Jefferson cited were obscure (the first twelve referred to events that often occurred within particular provinces, had not played prominent roles in the Americans' previous lists of grievances, and remained mysterious even to some well-informed contemporaries), technically inaccurate, or obviously overstated. The delegates, for example, removed "ships of war" from the clause charging George III with keeping military forces in the colonies without their legislatures' permission, probably because the colonial assemblies' jurisdiction over the sea was questionable. They also added the words "in many cases" to Jefferson's charge that the king had deprived the colonists of trial by jury since jury trials had not been snuffed out everywhere in America. Above all, however, Congress cut Jefferson's long, overwrought passage pinning responsibility for the slave trade on the king. That passage implicitly denied that the colonists had any responsibility for shipping Africans across the Atlantic and selling them as slaves, called attention to the existence of an American slave system clearly at odds with the documents' assertion that "all men are created equal," and insisted that George III's offer to free slaves who joined his cause proved that he was a tyrant. As written, the clause was simply unbelievable. The Declaration was stronger without it.

The Congress's most extensive editorial changes were made on the final half of the draft Declaration, which Jefferson probably wrote last and so had the least time to revise. His attack on the British people was, again, overlong, and it also lapsed at times into melodrama. The delegates cut it back to a marvelously succinct statement that ended, eloquently, by saying that henceforth the Americans would hold the British "as we hold the rest of mankind, enemies in war, in peace friends." The phrase was Jefferson's, but it had been all but lost in his draft, where it lay buried within a storm of words. Then the delegates thoroughly revised the document's final paragraph, inserting the moving words of the Lee resolution that it had adopted on July 2—"that these united colonies are and of right ought to be free and independent states"—in place of Jefferson's prose, appealing to "the supreme judge of the world for the rectitude of our intentions" and stating the Americans' "firm reliance on the protection of divine providence." Such references to God were conspicuously missing in Jefferson's final paragraph. However, Congress kept Jefferson's magnificent final words, by which, "for the support of this declaration," the delegates pledged to one another "our lives, our fortunes, and our sacred honor."

The Congress's editing was splendid; it created a document far stronger than Jefferson and the drafting committee submitted for consideration, although Jefferson didn't see it that way. (He made no fewer than six handwritten copies of the committee draft, marking in Congress's changes so correspondents could witness how it had "mutilated" his work.) Finally, on July 4, Congress laid down its pen and adopted the Declaration, which it ordered printed and sent out to be proclaimed before the army and in the states. Fifteen days later, after the New York legislature added its consent to the decision for independence, Congress resolved that "the Declaration passed on the 4th, be fairly engrossed on parchment, with the title and stile of 'the unanimous declaration of the thirteen United States of America,' and that the same, when engrossed, be signed by every member of Congress." The formal signing occurred on August 2—

although some members added their "John Hancocks" at later times.

Meanwhile, printed copies of the document circulated through the country, carrying the news that the United States had claimed "a separate and equal station" among "the powers of the earth." Since the Declaration of Independence provided "the Ground & Foundation" of a new American government, as a cover letter from the Congress's president, John Hancock, told the states, it should be proclaimed "in such a Manner, that the People may be universally informed of it."[17] And so the Declaration was reprinted in newspapers and broadsides and publicly read in both rural hamlets and seaport towns wherever the people assembled, characteristically accompanied by abundant huzzahs, militia demonstrations, and ceremonial shootings of guns and cannons.

Americans were celebrating independence, not the Declaration—the thing, not its announcement. In almost every instance, quotations of the Declaration came from its final paragraph—the one that actually declared America's separation from Britain with the words not of Thomas Jefferson but of another Virginian, Richard Henry Lee. Then, with the old regime formally dissolved, Americans went back to the hard work of creating new governments to take its place. And when, like Virginia, the states enacted declarations or bills of rights either as separate documents or as part of their new constitutions, they frequently turned, as Jefferson had, to the Mason draft of the Virginia Declaration of Rights. The Mason draft was widely republished and had a far greater influence on contemporary public writing than either the revised version that Virginia finally enacted or the Declaration of Independence. Not one state's declaration or bill of rights said "all men are created equal," but several said, with some minor variations, that "all men are born equally free and independent."[18] Eighteenth-century Americans, it seems, preferred Mason's over Jefferson's statement of men's fundamental equality and the principles behind the Revolution of 1776.

Indeed, few if any commentators outside Jefferson's immediate circle seemed to find the Declaration of Independence a particularly distinguished piece of writing. And once the Declaration had served its function, waving out King George and making way for the new republic, it was seldom read, even at Fourth of July celebrations, or even mentioned. Like a piece of fireworks, it spread a magnificent display over the land for a few brief moments, then flickered out and was gone—for almost twenty years.

II. THE CONSTITUTION

Americans were every bit as hesitant to create a new "American empire"—a national government with substantial power over the states—as they had been to leave the British Empire. Surely they were not prepared in 1776 to grant such a government powers they had recently denied Parliament, such as the power to tax and to regulate trade. Congress took two days to edit and adopt the Declaration of Independence, but more than a year to approve a much-revised and substantially weakened version of the Articles of Confederation first proposed by a drafting committee. Finally, on November 15, 1777, Congress adopted the document and asked the states to ratify it quickly, hopefully by March 10, 1778. But the

Articles of Confederation did not get the necessary unanimous consent of the states until March 1781—about eight months before the American victory at Yorktown and the end of the Revolutionary War.

No doubt the United States was better off under the Articles of Confederation, which bound the states together in a "perpetual union," than under the ad hoc government of the old Second Continental Congress. But was "better" good enough? By the time the Articles went into effect, some observers thought that the government the Articles created was already outmoded. The states' first constitutions, which were enacted between 1776 and 1780, had moved from creating governments in which power was heavily concentrated in the elected legislatures toward a greater separation and balancing of powers. But the "new" government under the Articles of Confederation consisted of a unicameral legislature that held legislative, executive, and judicial authority, as had the Second Continental Congress.[19] It looked like a throwback to the governments of 1776, which, given the rapid changes that occurred in American constitutionalism over the next five years, looked very old hat by 1781.

The states had also found a way to create constitutions based firmly on the sovereignty of the people, constitutions that were therefore different from the ordinary laws passed by state legislatures. In particular, the Massachusetts constitution of 1780, which many regarded as the most advanced of the series, was drafted by a special body of elected delegates meeting as a "constitutional convention." Then the people, meeting in their towns, ratified it. That made the constitution, as the Massachusetts constitution said, "a social compact, by which the whole people covenants with each citizen, and each citizen with the whole people, that all shall be governed by certain laws for the common good." Indeed, the Massachusetts constitution was in the most literal sense a creation of the people: "We . . . the people of Massachusetts," it said, " . . . do agree upon, ordain and establish, the following Declaration of Rights, and Frame of Government, as the CONSTITUTION of the COMMONWEALTH of MASSACHUSETTS."[20] In comparison, the "government" set up under the Articles of Confederation was no government at all, since it had no grant of authority from the people and could exert no power on the people themselves. It was a creature of the states, the administrative organ of a league of states—more like the League of Nations or United Nations of the twentieth century than a "true" government.

By the 1780s, there were reasons to regret the Confederation's weakness. It was unable to make Britain evacuate its old posts in the Northwest Territory, as Britain had promised to do under the Treaty of Paris, which concluded the Revolutionary War. The British were absolved from that obligation, they said, by American violations of the treaty. Congress had recommended that the states treat loyalists fairly, as the treaty specified, but several states ignored that recommendation. There was nothing Congress could do about that. And when Britain put up trade barriers against American imports, Congress could not retaliate because it had no power to tax imports. Indeed, it had no power to lay taxes of any sort, but could only "requisition" the states for funds— which, once the war was over, the states were often unwilling to pay. Efforts to give Congress the power to levy an "impost," or duty, on imports failed: since the Articles

of Confederation could not be amended without unanimous consent, the opposition of just one state could and
did block that relatively modest change—little Rhode
Island in 1781, and New York two years later. Soon it
seemed as if Congress would be unable to hold the territory to which the United States had title: would Kentucky
leave the Union and join Spain? Would Vermont become
part of Canada? Indeed, would the Confederation itself
gradually disappear? By the late 1780s, Congress had
trouble even attracting the quorum of delegates necessary
for it to act.

And yet, in April 1787, when James Madison, a thirty-
seven-year-old Virginian who was rapidly emerging as
the most reflective and influential nationalist, listed the
"vices" of the American political system, he was more
concerned with the wrongful acts of the states than with
the weaknesses of the Confederation. Time after time the
states had violated the Articles of Confederation, en-
croaching on federal authority and violating the rights of
each other. The states seemed caught up in an orgy of
lawmaking, which was itself "a pestilence," Madison
thought. Worse yet, many of the new laws passed by tri-
umphant state majorities violated the rights of minorities.
Just the creation of a new, substantively powerful national government would cut back or check the all-
pervasive power of the states, which their rambunctious
new governments seemed all too ready to use.[21]

Madison also concluded that the rights of the people
would be more reliably protected in a national government than by state governments. Because the nation
included so many different interests, it would be hard
for any one interest to dominate and oppress others.
Moreover, the nation would necessarily include a larger

population, and so have more men of ability, who could mediate conflicting interests among their constituents, than any single state. Big was better in "republican" governments, Madison thought.[22] That reversed the prevailing wisdom of the time, which said republics could work only over small areas.

Madison found an ally in Alexander Hamilton, a New Yorker who was even younger than he. Born in the West Indies, where he was orphaned before supporters had sent him to New York for an education, smart, and aware of his abilities, Hamilton was just thirty in 1787. But he had fought in the Revolutionary War, served for a time as Washington's adjutant, and became, like so many officers of the Continental Army, committed to creating a national government worthy of the name. He and a set of fellow nationalists, including Madison, saw their chance at Annapolis, Maryland, in September 1786, when only five delegations appeared at a convention called to discuss trade problems. Rather than simply dissolve, the runt meeting (remembered as the Annapolis Convention or Conference) decided to invite the states to send delegates to another convention, which would meet at Philadelphia on the second Monday of May 1787, to "take into consideration the situation of the United States," and "to devise such further provisions as shall appear to them necessary to render the constitution of the Federal Government adequate to the exigencies of the Union."[23]

Several states had already chosen delegates on February 21, 1787, when the Continental Congress endorsed the proposal. It was "expedient," Congress said, that a convention assemble "for the sole and express purpose of revising the Articles of Confederation" and proposing such alterations in the Articles as would, when agreed to by Congress and ratified by the states, "render the federal Constitution adequate to the exigencies of Government, and the preservation of the Union."[24] Revising the Articles was, however, a more limited task than what the Annapolis Convention had proposed. But by then events in Massachusetts, where a group of insurgents had risen up, closed courts, and, under the leadership of a Revolutionary War veteran named Daniel Shays, attacked the federal arsenal at Springfield, made revision or perhaps replacement of the Articles seem all the more urgent. Shays's rebellion was readily repressed in late January and early February 1787, but there were similar movements of the discontented in other states. Were they a sign of the anarchy that had historically led to the downfall of republics? Could anything be done to save the republic, and so the Revolution?

The delegates who assembled at Philadelphia were a notable lot. Fifty-five men out of the seventy-four delegates elected by the states attended the constitutional convention. In the almost eleven years since independence was declared, they had keenly observed the workings of the American government. Several had helped write state constitutions, and even if they had not, the delegates who met in Philadelphia were aware of institutional developments on the state level. The design of governments based on popular choice that, unlike the ephemeral republics of earlier times, could survive the rigors of time had become, they knew, the primary intellectual and practical challenge of their time. Seven delegates were then or had been governors of their states; others had served in state legislatures, and forty-two— about seventy-six percent—had been at one time or another delegates to the Continental Congress, so they knew the Confederation's strengths and weaknesses first-hand. Franklin, at age eighty-one, was by far the oldest delegate, and George Washington, at fifty-five, was one of the most senior members of the convention. The delegates' average age was forty-two or forty-three, but many of the movers and shakers were, like Madison and Hamilton, even younger. These were men who learned their politics within the institutions of the Revolution, not the colonial world; they knew the tricks of getting things done where the people, not a king, had ultimate power. And they would need every trick and insight they could conjure up: the convention, they had come to believe, would decide nothing less than the fate of republican government, and so the success or failure of the American Revolution.[25]

After assembling on May 25, the convention elected officers, making Washington its president and William Jackson secretary, and defined its rules of procedure. Its proceedings, the delegates decided, would be secret so they could debate freely and change their positions without public embarrassment. Then Virginia's governor, Edmund Randolph, rose, discussed the situation the convention confronted, and offered a plan for a completely revised national government.[26]

The Virginia Plan—which members of the Virginia delegation prepared while waiting for a quorum of state delegations to arrive—was not a draft constitution. It was a list of fifteen provisions, often with blank spaces for such items as the terms or age requirements for particular offices. Even so, it proposed that the national government have a bicameral legislature empowered to legislate "in all cases to which the separate States are incompetent, or

in which the harmony of the United States may be inter-
rupted" by a cacophony of state laws, and the power to
veto state laws and bring force against states that refused
to obey the new Constitution. Representation in the legislature, moreover, would be proportioned to population,
unlike in the current Continental Congress, where each
state had one vote regardless of how many people it held.
The Virginia Plan also called for a separate "National
Executive" and "National Judiciary." And it said the new
Constitution should be ratified by special state conventions elected by the people. It would therefore create a
substantive government, not a league of states.[27]

Immediately the convention turned to revising and ex-
panding the list of propositions Randolph presented. But
after two weeks, William Paterson of New Jersey, whose
delegation was uncomfortable with the convention's direction, presented an alternative plan. In fact, the government proposed by the New Jersey Plan was in many
aspects not all that different from the Virginia Plan. It
also would have a separate national executive and a national judiciary, and the national legislature would have
substantially greater power—including the powers to tax
and to regulate commerce. The legislature under the New
Jersey Plan would be unicameral, not bicameral, as Virginia suggested, and each state would have one vote, as
under the Articles of Confederation. But the laws of
Congress and treaties ratified under the power of the
United States would become "the supreme law of the respective States" and the federal executive could use force
in compelling obedience to those laws and treaties.[28]

The New Jersey Plan took the form of amendments to
the Articles of Confederation. That, its proponents insisted, was all the convention was authorized to do.

Paterson said the delegates' object was not to create "such a Government as may be best in itself, but such a one as our Constituents have authorized us to prepare, and as they will approve."[29] But to amend the Articles required unanimous consent—and Rhode Island had not even deigned to send delegates to the Philadelphia convention. Paterson's proposal was therefore hopeless, and the delegates had no trouble rejecting it, by a vote of 7 to 3, on June 19.

They were also apparently less than excited by another plan, presented by Hamilton, that would have placed "compleat sovereignty" in a central government, reducing the states to administrative units of the nation. That, the delegates understood, would have no chance of being ratified, as, it seems, did Hamilton, who did not offer his scheme of government as a formal proposal.[30] And so the delegates went back to work on the Virginia Plan. That meant they would propose a complete break with the Articles of Confederation—but one that would carve out a middle way between the current system, in which states held all real power, and another, in which power was concentrated in the nation.

Rejecting the New Jersey Plan did not, however, settle the issue of representation, over which the convention came close to dissolving. The Virginians and other states that either had high populations or expected their populations to grow dramatically insisted that representation in a republic had to be proportioned to population so each person had roughly equal power. That principle was basic to republican government, they said. It had been "improperly violated" in the Articles of Confederation, and they could not accept any new plan of government that did not repair the defect. "Are not the Citizens of

Pen[nsylvania] equal to those of N[ew] Jersey?" Penn-sylvania's James Wilson asked; "does it require 150 of the former to balance 50 of the latter?" The delegates of small states such as Delaware were equally adamant. They were bound by their instructions, they said, to op-pose any plan that did not give the states equal voting power. Finally, on July 16, a compromise proposed by Connecticut settled the controversy. Each state would have equal power in the Senate, but both representation in the House of Representatives and taxes would be pro-portioned to a state's free population, including servants, and three-fifths of "all other Persons" except "Indians not taxed."[31]

The "other persons" were slaves. Why should they be represented at all, since they didn't vote or pay taxes? If slaves were, as the South insisted, property, why weren't other forms of property—New England's cows, for ex-ample—also represented? The delegates from the South wanted slaves counted equally with white people not be-cause they considered blacks equal to whites, but because that would increase the power of white Southerners. Others preferred that slaves not be counted at all, but ended up accepting the three-fifths figure—which came from a congressional resolution of April 18, 1783—as a compromise. Once that issue was settled, the basic agree-ment among delegates on the direction of change allowed the convention to proceed relatively smoothly.

By July 26, the fifteen resolutions of the Virginia Plan had grown to twenty-three that laid out the basic struc-ture of the new government. At that point the convention recessed until August 6, while a "Committee of Detail" reworked the resolutions into a draft Constitution. Then the debates resumed until September 8, when the delegates elected a "Committee of Style" to revise and re-arrange the revised Articles into a more finished form. Four days later that committee submitted a draft Constitution that began—in words strikingly like those of the Massachusetts constitution of 1780—"We, the people of the United States...do ordain and establish this Constitution of the United States of America." And, again like Massachusetts, the organization of the document reflected that of the government it created. Article I was on the legislative; Article II on the executive, and Article III on the judicial power. Four additional Articles prescribed the rights of states and their citizens in relation to each other, explained how new states could be admitted to the Union, and guaranteed every state "a Republican form of government"; defined procedures for amending the Constitution; declared the Constitution, laws, and treaties made under the authority of the United States—in words that recalled the New Jersey Plan—"the supreme law of the land," binding on officials of both the United States and the individual states, and said the Constitution would be ratified when approved by conventions in nine member states. Unanimity would not be necessary; and once nine states ratified, the decision in the others would be not whether they liked the proposed Constitution, but whether they'd stay in or leave the Union—which was easier to decide in the affirmative. The delegates continued revising or adding to the draft Constitution on through Monday, September 17, 1787, when they approved an important change in the provision on representation. Then, some four months after the convention first convened, thirty-nine delegates signed a parchment copy of, in Madison's words, "the constitution, as finally amended," and adjourned.

The final Constitution was not just longer but substantially different from the Virginia Plan. It set up a bicameral legislature, the Congress, in which members of one body, the House of Representatives, were chosen for two-year terms "by the people of the several States." Representation there would be proportioned to population and adjusted according to a decennial census. The other house, the Senate, consisted of two delegates from each state elected by their state legislatures (not, as the Virginia Plan said, by the "first branch" of the legislature from persons nominated by the states' legislatures). Senators served for six-year terms, with a third of the membership coming up for election every two years. The powers of Congress were stated in detail, and included the power to tax and to regulate both foreign and domestic commerce as well as an omnibus power to "make all laws...necessary and proper" for executing the other powers assigned to it.

One person, "a President of the United States of America," was entrusted with the executive power. (Edmund Randolph, who presented the Virginia Plan, thought the executive power should be in a committee, which could act less decisively than a single individual.) In 1776, the word "president" referred to a weak executive, a person who presided over a meeting; "governor" implied a strong executive. But this "president" had substantial powers. He would be commander in chief of the American army and navy as well as of the state militias; with the "advice and consent of the Senate" he could conclude treaties and appoint ambassadors, judges, and other officers of the United States, and recommend to Congress measures he considered "necessary and expedient." He even had some powers over the convening and adjourning of Congress.

After it invested more and more responsibilities in the president, the convention had reduced his term of office from seven years, which at one point seemed appropriate, to four. The Constitution also provided for a vice president, elected with the president and for the same term of office, who would preside over the Senate. If the president died, resigned, was unable to "discharge the powers and duties of his office," or was removed from office, the vice president would become president. How should the president and vice president be elected? That was one of the most difficult issues the convention faced. Some delegates thought the people should elect them— but would the people have sufficient information about candidates from distant parts of the country? That seemed so doubtful that the task was entrusted to an idiosyncratic "electoral college," whose structure and procedures were prescribed in detail (see Article II, Section 1, paragraph 3).

Neither the members of the House of Representatives, senators, nor the president and vice president were subject to property qualifications for office, such as many state constitutions prescribed. Officers under the new Constitution needed only to fulfill requirements of age, residency, and citizenship. The president, for example, had to be a "natural born Citizen, or a Citizen of the United States, at the time of the adoption of this Constitution." (The last provision was added to satisfy delegates such as Pennsylvania's James Wilson, an immigrant from Scotland, who objected to being excluded from high office by a constitution he had helped write.) The president also had to be thirty-five years of age and have been a resident of the United States for at least fourteen years. In that way, the door of opportunity was swung wide open: any capable white male citizen who had lived within the United States for the requisite period could aspire to the estimable age of thirty-five and so qualify for the presidency. The provision reflected the confidence of the revolutionary generation that merit alone should determine who held office, and both age and residency provided rough measures of experience and knowledge of the United States—not family or personal wealth, which was understood to be a bad measure of merit. (Some of the greatest rogues he ever knew, Franklin told the convention, were the richest rogues.)

Article III of the Constitution, on the judiciary, was far briefer than its predecessors. It placed the judicial power of the United States in "one Supreme Court, and in such inferior courts as the Congress may from time to time ordain and establish." The judges would hold their offices on good behavior and their salaries could not be reduced while they remained on the bench—which was meant to free them from manipulation by the executive and legislature. The federal courts had jurisdiction over issues raised under the Constitution and over laws and treaties of the United States: the government of the United States would not be dependent on state courts for the enforcement of its powers.

Each unit of the new government had a distinct task—to make, execute, or enforce the laws. The lines between those divisions were, however, not hard and fast. The president, after all, could veto laws, and members of the Senate had to approve many executive appointments. But no member of the legislative, executive, or judicial branches of the new federal government could hold office in the other two, which distinguished "separation of powers" in the United States. In Britain, for example, cabinet officers were customarily drawn from the House of Lords or the House of Commons. Separation of powers was one way the constitutional convention tried to avoid a dangerous concentration of authority that would, they feared, threaten American liberty.

So did the division of power between the federal and state governments. Both levels of government received distinct and complementary spheres of authority from the sovereign people; both were limited by the existence of the other. The Constitution imposed some explicit limitations on the states: Article I, Section 10 said they could not do a series of things such as "make anything but gold and silver coin a tender in payment of debts" or impair the obligation of contracts (as they had often done in the 1780s, interfering with the rights of creditors), grant titles of nobility, or pass bills of attainder or ex post facto laws. The earlier word for such a composite government was "empire," but that word seemed inappropriate for a system in which the states were not strictly subordinate to the central government and had independent authority of their own. Gradually the government of the United States became known instead as a "federal" system.

One measure of how much the constitutional convention did lies in the dissatisfaction of those responsible for the Virginia Plan. Madison thought the Constitution included several fatal errors, above all its violation of proportional representation in the Senate. (He had no idea that in the nineteenth century the Senate would become the protector of Southern rights and a check against Northern majoritarian "tyranny"—just the kind of device Madison had kept seeking.) He also thought the convention's unwillingness to let Congress veto state laws that contravened the Constitution or federal treaties was a big mistake. Madison had no confidence that the federal courts would do that job effectively.[32] His kinsman, Edmund Randolph, who had introduced the Virginia Plan, was so unhappy with the convention's work, and particularly with what he called "the indefinite and dangerous power given...to Congress" that he refused to sign the document. So did his fellow Virginian George Mason as well as Elbridge Gerry of Massachusetts.

Other delegates also had objections, but took the advice that Franklin gave in a speech read for him by James Wilson. "I confess," he began, "that there are several parts of this constitution which I do not at present approve," but "having lived long, I have experienced many instances of being obliged by better information, or fuller consideration, to change opinions even on important subjects...." As a result, Franklin said,

I agree to this Constitution with all its faults, if they are such; because I think a general Government necessary for us, and there is no form of Government but what may be a blessing to the people if well administered.... I doubt too whether any other Convention we can obtain, may be able to make a better Constitution. For when you assemble a number of men to have the advantage of their joint wisdom, you inevitably assemble with those men, all their prejudices, their passions, their errors of opinion, their local interests, and their selfish views. From such an assembly can a perfect production be expected? It therefore astonishes me...to find this system approaching so near to perfection as it does;

and I think it will astonish our enemies, who are waiting with confidence to hear that our councils are confounded like those of the Builders of Babel.... Thus I consent...to this Constitution because I expect no better, and because I am not sure, that it is not the best. The opinions I have had of its errors, I sacrifice to the public good.

And he called on other delegates with objections to the Constitution to "doubt a little of his infallibility."[33]

Few if any expected the Constitution to last two hundred years, much less find its way onto an "altar" in the National Archives. If the new Constitution didn't work, however, it could later be amended or replaced. After all, some states had already replaced their first, revolutionary state constitutions with others that were, hopefully, built more skillfully than their predecessors. Revolutionary America produced the first written constitutions the world had ever seen, and accumulated extraordinary insight into the science of institutional design in the eleven years since independence. Who could think that the process of learning had ended? The Constitution of 1787 was built on the previous experience of the states as well as that of the Confederation. Before a better constitution could be written, it would have to be tried; the experiment needed to be run and the results taken into account.

That required getting the document ratified, which was no sure thing. Once the convention announced its proposal, the basic agreement, evident in the similarities between the Virginia and New Jersey plans, which allowed the delegates to work together with relative harmony, suddenly disappeared. The fight over ratification was one of the most divisive in all of American history.

III. THE BILL OF RIGHTS

On September 12, 1787, soon after the Committee of Style circulated copies of its draft Constitution, George Mason noticed a serious omission. He wished, he said, that "the plan had been prefaced with a Bill of Rights, & would second a motion if made for the purpose. It would give great quiet to the people; and with the aid of the State declarations, a bill might be prepared in a few hours." Gerry moved that the convention appoint a committee to prepare a bill of rights, and Mason, as promised, seconded the motion. But not one state delegation voted "aye."[34] The lack of a bill of rights was one reason Mason and Gerry refused to sign the document. Gerry said he wished that the Constitution had been presented "in a more mediating shape, in order to abate the heat and opposition of parties." As it stood, he feared that the Constitution would provoke such fierce opposition that a civil war could result.[35]

Why, then, was there so little support for Mason's idea? Perhaps the delegates were exhausted after struggling through a long, hot summer and wanted to finish their work and go home—except that they were willing to make other changes in the Constitution. Perhaps they thought that a bill of rights modeled on those of the states would include some variation on Mason's words of 1776, that "all men are born equally free and independent," which would alienate slaveholders and make ratification of the Constitution even more difficult. Virginia had already seen the inconsistency between those words and the institution of slavery in June 1776 and altered Mason's draft to try to get around the problem; later, some slaves won their freedom in Massachusetts courts by arguing that the words "all men are born free and independent" in the Massachusetts Declaration of Rights was incompatible with slavery.[36] Or perhaps, like Madison, they thought "parchment barriers" were not worth the ink it took to write them. Declarations of rights had not kept state legislatures from violating the people's rights during the 1780s, he noted. The only effective way to protect freedom, Madison believed, was by building checks on power into the structure of the government—as the new Constitution did. Since the new government was one of limited powers, it did not have powers that weren't mentioned in the Constitution. That meant there was no need to say, for example, that Congress could not interfere with freedom of speech: since Congress wasn't explicitly given that power, it obviously could not interfere with freedom of speech. Indeed, bills of rights could do more harm than good if they implied that the people had only the rights they listed, that rights unmentioned were not rights at all.[37]

Politically, however, it was a big blunder not to combine a bill of rights with the new Constitution. The Anti-Federalists, who opposed ratification of the Constitution, had a substantial arsenal of arguments to show that the Constitution would undermine, not save, republican government, that it was essentially a step back to all the Americans had rejected in 1776, but they seldom failed to mention the lack of a bill of rights. Several states combined their ratification of the Constitution with a list of amendments that they thought should be enacted once it went into effect. Those lists always included provisions protecting basic rights. Without the device of recommending amendments, it is doubtful whether the Constitution would have been adopted. Indeed, Virginia's ratification resolution included a statement that "no right of any denomination can be canceled, abridged, restrained, or modified" by the new federal government "except in those instances in which power is given by the Constitution for those purposes: and that among other essential rights the liberty of Conscience and of the Press cannot be canceled, abridged, restrained, or modified by any authority of the United States." It also declared that the powers granted under the Constitution could be resumed by the people "whensover the same shall be perverted to their injury or oppression." Virginians obviously had very little confidence in the new Constitution.[38]

Anti-Federalist sentiment in Virginia was, in fact, so strong that Madison failed to win a place in the Senate. He settled for a seat in the House of Representatives, but to get that he had to assure the voters that he would support amendments to the Constitution.[39] The wisdom in conciliating the Constitution's opponents seemed to him reason enough to do that. An exchange of letters with Thomas Jefferson, then the American minister in Paris, who argued strongly for a bill of rights, also softened Madison's opposition.[40]

And so, on June 8, 1789, Madison moved in the first federal Congress that "a declaration" be "prefixed to the constitution." That "prefix"—which seems to have constituted what Madison called a "bill of rights"—would say

That all power is originally vested in, and consequently derived from the people.

That Government is instituted, and ought to be exercised for the benefit of the people; which consists in the enjoyment of life and liberty, with the right of acquiring and using property, and generally of pursuing and obtaining happiness and safety.

That the people have an indubitable, unalienable, and indefeasible right to reform or change their government, whenever it be found adverse or inadequate to the purposes of its institution.

Madison also proposed making a long list of changes in the body of the Constitution. For example, he wanted the provision on representation in Article I, Section 2, clause 3 changed so it would no longer say that the number of representatives "shall not exceed one for every thirty thousand," which one Anti-Federalist after another condemned as a violation of the people's right to full and free representation in Congress. And he wanted Article I, Section 6, clause 1 to say that no law increasing the compensation of representatives could take effect before another election had taken place. More important, he proposed inserting into Article I, Section 9 of the Constitution, which imposed restrictions on Congress's powers, provisions protecting several basic rights, including freedom of religion, of speech, and of the press, the rights of assembly and of petition, the right to bear arms, and a series of rights in criminal prosecutions. His proposals would specifically forbid excessive bail, "cruel and unusual punishments," "unreasonable searches and seizures," warrants issued without probable cause, and the deprivation of "life, liberty, or property without due process of law." Madison also wanted a statement that "no state shall violate the equal rights of conscience, or the freedom of the press, or the trial by jury in criminal cases" added to Article I, Section 10.[41]

What Madison proposed was not what the country got. The Federalists who dominated the first federal Congress saw no reason to change the Constitution so soon, and, in any case, considered other issues as far more urgent. The Constitution, after all, left a lot of institution-designing to the new government itself: Congress, for example, had to work out the details of the new federal judiciary and also the executive branch and the relation of cabinet officers (about which the Constitution said nothing) to the legislature. Finally, on September 28, 1789, after Madison's proposal was revised by the House, the Senate, and a conference committee, Congress sent to the states for ratification twelve proposed amendments. They would be listed at the end of the Constitution because Representative Roger Sherman of Connecticut insisted that Congress could not alter the body of the Constitution, which had been ratified by the people. Congress, with the consent of three-quarters of the states, could enact as legislative acts only those amendments that were "detached from the constitution and . . . supplementary to it."[42] That, however, made the new amendments look like afterthoughts, which of course they were.

Then the states approved only ten of the twelve amendments, rejecting the first two on Congress's list— one concerned with representation, the other (which was finally enacted in 1992 as the Twenty-seventh Amendment) saying that any change in the compensation paid to senators and representatives could take effect only after an election intervened. The ten became, in December 1791, the federal Bill of Rights, a bare-bones lawyer's list of rights with two additional provisions: the Ninth Amendment declared that the previous statement of rights "shall not be construed to deny or disparage others retained by the people"; the Tenth Amendment said that powers which the Constitution did not delegate to the United States or prohibit to the states were "reserved to the States respectively, or to the people." The federal Bill of Rights lacked any of the natural-rights flourishes so common in the state documents. Nor did it include any of the structural changes in the federal government that Anti-Federalists wanted—checks on federal taxation power, for example, or the creation of a special executive council to assume the Senate's role in advising and consenting to various executive actions. And not everyone was happy with it. The Bill of Rights, one congressman complained, was little better than "whip syllabub," a popular eighteenth-century dessert, "frothy and full of wind, formed only to please the palate, or they are like a tub thrown out to a whale" at sea to divert it from doing damage to a ship, and so "secure the freight of the ship and its peaceable voyage."[43]

What, in fact, did the Bill of Rights do? On that, Madison's proposal was reasonably clear: some provisions restricted Congress, others the states. The First Amendment of the Bill of Rights as enacted said "Congress shall make no law respecting an establishment of religion, or prohibiting the free exercise thereof; or abridging the freedom of speech, or of the press; or the right of the people peaceably to assemble, and to petition the Government for a redress of grievances." But no subsequent amendment began in the same way. Instead, subsequent amendments were written as general edicts. The Second Amendment, for example, said "A well-regulated militia, being necessary to the security of a free State, the right of the people to keep and bear arms, shall not be infringed." If the amendments were part of the

Constitution, which was "the supreme Law of the Land" (Article VI), all such general principles should have been binding on the states as well as on the federal government. Indeed, one argument for a federal bill of rights lay in its capacity to remedy the inconsistency in state laws by providing a general, uniform foundation for Americans' basic rights. But in 1833 the Supreme Court under Chief Justice John Marshall decided, in the case of *Barron* v. *The Mayor of Baltimore,* that the federal Bill of Rights restricted only the federal government. Even there it didn't prove particularly effective: in the late 1790s, for example, when the Federalists passed a sedition law that seemed clearly to violate the First Amendment, the courts did not interfere—in part because the judges were almost entirely Federalists. In any case, in the early republic the federal government remained substantially less significant than the states, so checking its already insubstantial authority was not a critical function. Immediately after its enactment, in short, the federal Bill of Rights, if not forgotten, as the Declaration of Independence had been, was anything but a revered and important document.

Its resurrection, in fact, turned in a curious way on the history of the Declaration of Independence, which began its rise from obscurity soon after the Bill of Rights was ratified. Since neither the federal Constitution nor the Bill of Rights said anything about men being born (or created) equal or having inalienable (or unalienable) rights, persons who continued to believe in the relevance of those ideas—and who found them useful in national politics—had to cite the Declaration of Independence. It was all they had. And so, in the 1790s, that old revolutionary manifesto began a rather dramatic comeback.

Members of the "Republican Party" began celebrating it as the work of Thomas Jefferson, one of their leaders. That it had some distant resemblance to France's Declaration of the Rights of Man (1789) didn't hurt either: the Republicans were friends of France and its Revolution, while Federalists turned sour on France after the execution of Louis XVI and the onset of the Terror. And when the Republicans quoted the Declaration of Independence, their citations came not from the last paragraph, but the second, the one that said "all men are created equal" and have "certain unalienable rights...."

What began as a Republican property became a national icon after the War of 1812, when a new generation of Americans looked back to the Revolution with awe, tried desperately to preserve the memories, relics, and documents of that time, and turned the Founding Fathers into supermen and their written testaments into holy writ. In this new role as a form of scripture, the Declaration of Independence proved very useful to one cause after another—that of workers, or women, or farmers, who felt that their equality or rights were being violated. The cause that claimed its authority most powerfully, however, was that of abolitionism: if men were "created equal," that is, if no man was born with authority over another, if all legitimate authority came from consent, as the Declaration said, slavery was profoundly wrong.

Slavery's defenders answered by questioning the principle itself. Men were not, they said, "born" or "created" equal. How "equal" was a baby to his or her parents? Nature, they argued, put people from the beginning in a situation of subordination, and only then could they grow, learn, and develop their capacities. Too bad the

Declaration of Independence included such a self-evident falsehood, even a "self-evident lie," especially since the United States could easily have declared its independence without it.[44]

There was, however, a body of Americans, raised on post-1815 patriotic rhetoric, who found such arguments deeply offensive. They believed they had an obligation to protect and continue the tradition of the Revolution, not to reject or denounce it. Eventually these men would find a political home in a new Republican Party of the 1850s. They took on the defense of the Declaration and its principles, which gradually assumed an entirely new function—not as a revolutionary manifesto, but as a statement of principles to guide an established government, like a bill of rights.

Abraham Lincoln expressed the views of this group with great power and eloquence. For him—as for other onetime Whigs who became Republicans—the Declaration of Independence's provision on equality was a sacred principle. What did it mean? Not that men were alike in *"all respects."* The nation's founders "did not mean to say all were equal in size, intellect, moral development, or social capacity." What they said was that men were equal in having "certain unalienable rights, among which are life, liberty, and the pursuit of happiness," Lincoln said, and that they meant. Nor did the founders mean to say "that all were then actually enjoying that equality, nor yet, that they were about to confer it immediately upon them." Clearly they could not. The revolutionaries could not right all wrongs at once. What they meant to do in the Declaration of Independence, Lincoln said, was simply to declare the *right* so that the *enforcement* of it might follow as fast as circumstances should permit. They meant to set up a standard maxim for free society, which should be familiar to all, and revered by all; constantly looked to, and constantly labored for, and even though never perfectly attained, constantly approximated, and thereby constantly spreading and deepening its influence, and augmenting the happiness and value of life to all people of all colors everywhere.[45]

That was, indeed, a radical interpretation of the Declaration of Independence, one that went far beyond anything Thomas Jefferson could imagine: Jefferson, after all, doubted that whites and free black Americans could live together in peace, much less on a basis of equality, within the United States. And Lincoln's position was not his alone. He shared his devotion to the Declaration, he said, with his constituents, particularly those who were immigrants and regarded the Declaration's assertion that "all men are created equal" as "the father of all moral principle[s]" because it made them one with all other Americans.[46] He also shared his position with other members of the Republican Party, who wrote the principles stated in the Declaration of Independence into their platform in 1856 and 1860.[47] More important, after the end of the Civil War, and after Lincoln's death, Republicans enacted the Thirteenth Amendment to the Constitution, which ended slavery and involuntary servitude; the Fourteenth Amendment, which precluded the states from abridging "the privileges or immunities of citizens of the United States" or depriving "any person of life, liberty, or property, without due process of law; nor deny to any person within its jurisdiction the equal protection of the laws"; and the Fifteenth Amendment, which said the right of American citizens to the vote could not be "denied or abridged by the United States or by any State on account of race, color, or previous condition of servitude." Those amendments served in some measure to read, finally, the principles of the Declaration of Independence into the Constitution.

At first the Fourteenth and Fifteenth amendments made little difference. But in the twentieth century, the Supreme Court began using the Fourteenth Amendment to make the states respect the Bill of Rights. The earliest cases concerned free speech; later, the Fourteenth Amendment and Bill of Rights supported cases against racial segregation, malapportionment of representation, and the rights of criminals. Finally, thanks to the Fourteenth Amendment— the work of nineteenth-century Republicans who believed deeply in the Declaration of Independence—the Bill of Rights became a powerful protector of Americans' rights.[48] And, not surprisingly, the discovery of the parchment "Bill of Rights"—actually Congress's official copy of the twelve amendments it recommended to the states— coincided with the Bill of Rights' increasing importance in American law. The document joined the Declaration and the Constitution on the "Freedom Train," which toured the nation in September 1947 and January 1949, and later made its way to the altar in the National Archives.[49]

*   *   *

The story of the Americans' "founding documents" is not a simple one: documents once lost were later rediscovered. The Constitution's importance was never in doubt, but the Declaration of Independence underwent a massive redefinition and rise in importance in the late eighteenth and early nineteenth centuries. And the Bill of Rights in particular piggybacked its way to prominence on the Declaration of Independence, or, more precisely, on an amendment to the Constitution passed in part to realize the Declaration's principles.

Moreover, not one of those documents was the work of a single great man. Americans remember Thomas Jefferson as the author of the Declaration of Independence, and James Madison as the "father" of the Constitution and the Bill of Rights. But all three of those documents were adopted in forms different from what Jefferson and Madison proposed and preferred. They were created by bodies of men who spoke for their constituents, the American people, and were ratified by the people either directly or through their elected representatives. That made the "founding documents" of the United States different from their English predecessors, such as the Magna Charta, which were granted by kings to their subjects.

The future of those "founding documents" and the traditions they represent is also in the hands of the American people, who can begin to exercise their responsibilities in no better way than knowing what those "sacred texts" actually say. Happy reading!

—Pauline Maier
March 1998

NOTES

---

[1] In Madison, "Charters," an essay published in the *National Gazette* on January 18, 1792, in Robert A. Rutland, ed., *The Papers of James Madison,* XIV (Charlottesville, Va.: University Press of Virginia, 1983), 192.

[2] The text is available in Lois G. Schwoerer, *The Declaration of Rights, 1689* (Baltimore and London, 1981), Appendix I, 295–98, and also Jack Rakove, *Declaring Rights: A Brief History with Documents* (New York: St. Martin's Press, 1998), 41–45.

[3] Madison, "Charters," in Rutland, ed., *Madison Papers,* XIV, 191–92.

[4] The account of the development of independence here is based upon Pauline Maier, *American Scripture: Making the Declaration of Independence* (New York: Knopf, 1997).

[5] Buckingham County, Virginia, Instructions, [May 13, 1776?] in ibid., 226–29, esp. 228.

[6] Cited in ibid., 41.

[7] From Adams's autobiography, written about 1805, cited in ibid., 99.

[8] See Julian Boyd, ed., *The Papers of Thomas Jefferson,* I (Princeton, N.J.: Princeton University Press, 1950), 417–20.

[9] The citations here are to the draft as Jefferson first submitted it to the drafting committee, as it appears in Carl L. Becker, *Declaration of Independence: A Study in the History of Political Ideas* (New York: Vintage, 1953; orig. 1922), 141–51, and sometimes to the draft as it emerged from the committee. One reconstruction of that draft (which has been lost) is in ibid., 160–71, and, with emendations Congress made, 174–84. For another similar version of the committee draft with Congress's changes, see Maier, *American Scripture,* Appendix C, 235–41.

[10]See Maier, *American Scripture,* 135, and Stephen E. Lucas, "Justifying America: The Declaration of Independence as a Rhetorical Document," in Thomas W. Benson, ed., *American Rhetoric: Context and Criticism* (Carbondale, Ill.: Illinois University Press, 1989), 67–130, esp. 84.

[11]For Jefferson's final draft of the Virginia preamble, see Boyd, ed., *Jefferson Papers,* I, 356–57, and for the version Virginia adopted, which is quoted here, 377–79.

[12]See Maier, *American Scripture,* 133–34, and, for the first three clauses of the Mason draft, 126–27. The version cited there is from the *Pennsylvania Gazette* for June 12, 1776.

[13]Ibid., 104, and Stephen E. Lucas, "The Plakkaat Van Verlatinge: A Neglected Model for the American Declaration of Independence," in Rosemarijn J. Hoefte and Johanna C. Kardux, *Connecting Cultures: The Netherlands in Five Centuries of Transatlantic Exchange* (Amsterdam: VU University Press, 1994), esp. 203–07.

[14]See esp. "Jefferson to Madison, August 30, 1823," in Paul Leicester Ford, ed., *The Writings of Thomas Jefferson,* X (New York and London, 1899), 267–69.

[15]"Jefferson to Franklin, Friday morn. [June 21, 1776?]," in Boyd, ed., *Jefferson Papers,* I, 404.

[16]For these and changes discussed in the following paragraphs, see the committee report with Congress's editings in Maier, *American Scripture,* Appendix C, 236–41.

[17]"Hancock to Certain States, Philadelphia, July 6, 1776," in Paul H. Smith, ed., *Letters of Delegates to Congress, 1774–1789,* IV (Washington: U.S. Government Printing Office, 1979), 396.

[18]Maier, *American Scripture,* 164–67.

[19]The Articles of Confederation are reprinted in several places, including Samuel Eliot Morison, ed., *Sources and Documents Illustrating the American Revolution, 1764–1788, and the Formation of the Federal Constitution,* 2nd ed. (New York and London: Oxford University Press, 1929), 178–86.

[20]The text is available in Oscar and Mary Handlin, eds., *The Popular Sources of Political Authority: Documents on the Massachusetts Constitution of 1780* (Cambridge, 1966), 441–42.

[21]Madison, "Vices of the Political System of the United States," in Rutland, ed., *Madison Papers,* IX, 345–58.

[22]The argument, which Madison would later develop in the 10th Federalist Paper, is stated in his "Vices," ibid., 355–57.

[23]Cited in Christopher Collier and James Lincoln Collier, *Decision in Philadelphia: The Constitutional Convention of 1787* (New York: Ballantine, 1986), 32.

[24]*Journals of the Continental Congress,* XXXII (Washington, 1936), 74.

[25]Collier and Collier, *Decision in Philadelphia,* 76–78, and Max Farrand, *The Framing of the Constitution of the United States* (New Haven: Yale University Press, 1962; orig. 1913), 38–39. The significance of the nationalist/Federalist leaders' youth is discussed in Stanley Elkins and Eric McKitrick, "The Founding Fathers: Young Men of the Revolution," *Political Science Quarterly,* LXXVI (1961), 181–216, see also John Roche, "The Founding Fathers: A Reform Caucus in Action," on their skill at democratic politics, in *American Political Science Review,* LV (1961), 799–816.

[26]The account of the convention here is based to a considerable extent on Adrienne Koch, ed., *Notes of Debates in the Federal Convention of 1787 Reported by James Madison* (New York and London, 1987).

[27]Ibid., 30–33.

[28]Ibid., 118–21.

[29]Ibid., 122–23.

[30]Ibid., 138–39. Hamilton said he did not mean to offer his sketch of a government as "a proposition to the Committee" of the whole, but meant "only to give a more correct view of his ideas, and to suggest the amendments which he should probably propose to the plan of Mr. R[andolph] in the proper stages of its future discussion" (137). There was therefore no actual vote on his plan.

[31]Ibid., 97, 297–98.

[32]"Madison to Jefferson, September 6 and October 24, 1787," in Rutland, ed., *Madison Papers,* X, 163–64 (the Constitution "will neither effectually answer its national object nor prevent the local

mischiefs which everywhere excite disgusts ag[ain]st the state government") and 212–14.

[33]Madison, *Notes on Debates,* Koch, ed., 652–54.

[34]Ibid., 630.

[35]Ibid., 657–58.

[36]John E. Selby, *The Revolution in Virginia, 1775–1783* (Williamsburg, Va.: University Press of Virginia, 1988), 106–08; Arthur Zilversmit, *The First Emancipation: The Abolition of Slavery in the North* (Chicago and London, 1967), 112–15.

[37] "Madison to Jefferson, October 17, 1788," in Rutland, ed., *Madison Papers,* XI, 295–300.

[38]In Morison, ed., *Sources and Documents,* 362.

[39]See Rutland, ed., *Madison Papers,* XI, 301–04.

[40]The Jefferson-Madison correspondence is in Rutland, ed., *Madison Papers,* X and XI, and excerpts are also conveniently reprinted, with useful analysis, in Jack N. Rakove, *Declaring Rights: A Brief History with Documents* (Boston and New York, 1998), 147–66.

[41]Madison, speech of June 8, 1789, in ibid., 170–82, and Rutland, ed., *Madison Papers,* XII, 196–210.

[42]Rakove, *Declaring Rights,* 182, and Sherman's statement in House of Representatives, August 13, 1789, in Helen E. Veit et al., eds., *Creating the Bill of Rights: The Documentary Record from the First Federal Convention* (Baltimore and London: Johns Hopkins, 1991), 105.

[43] "Aedanus Burke, August 19, 1789," in Veit et al., eds., *Creating the Bill of Rights,* 175, and also cited in Rakove, *Declaring Rights,* 168.

[44]This account is, in general, drawn from Maier, *American Scripture,* ch. 4, in which the pro-slavery argument is described on pp. 199–200.

[45]Ibid, 200–208, including Lincoln citations, at 205–06, from a speech at Springfield, Illinois, June 26, 1857, available in Roy P. Basler, *Abraham Lincoln: His Speeches and Writings* (Cleveland and New York: Da Capo, 1946), 360–61.

[46]Lincoln's speech at Chicago, July 10, 1858, in ibid., 401–02.

[47]John Tweedy, *A History of the Republican National Conventions from 1856 to 1908* (Danbury, Connecticut, 1910), 16, 43–45.

[48]Rakove, *Declaring Rights,* 194–96, offers an admirably succinct summary of this development based in part upon Richard C. Cortner, *The Supreme Court and the Second Bill of Rights: The Fourteenth Amendment and the Nationalization of Civil Liberties* (Madison, Wisc.: University of Wisconsin Press, 1981) and David J. Bodenhamer and James W. Ely, Jr., eds., *The Bill of Rights in Modern America: After 200 Years* (Bloomington and Indianapolis, Ind.: Indiana University Press, 1993). See also Bernard Schwartz, *The Great Rights of Mankind: A History of the American Bill of Rights,* expanded edition (Madison, Wisc.: Madison House, 1992), esp. 202–225, and William J. Brennan, Jr., "The Bill of Rights and the States: The Revival of State Constitutions as Guardians of Individual Rights" in Norman Dorsen, ed., *The Evolving Constitution: Essays on the Bill of Rights and the U.S. Supreme Court* (Middletown, Conn.: University Press of New England, 1987), 254–70, 341–44.

[49]See Michael Kammen, *A Machine That Would Go of Itself: The Constitution in American Culture* (New York: St. Martin's Press, 1987), 336–56.

THE DECLARATION OF INDEPENDENCE

Action of Second Continental Congress, July 4, 1776
The unanimous Declaration of the thirteen
United States of America

WHEN IN the Course of human Events, it becomes necessary for one People to dissolve the Political Bands which have connected them with another, and to assume among the Powers of the Earth, the separate and equal Station to which the Laws of Nature and of Nature's God entitle them, a decent Respect to the Opinions of Mankind requires that they should declare the causes which impel them to the Separation.

WE hold these Truths to be self-evident, that all Men are created equal, that they are endowed by their Creator with certain unalienable Rights, that among these are Life, Liberty, and the Pursuit of Happiness—That to secure these Rights, Governments are instituted among Men, deriving their just Powers from the Consent of the Governed, that whenever any Form of Government becomes destructive of these Ends, it is the Right of the People to alter or to abolish it, and to institute new Government, laying its Foundation on such Principles, and organizing its Powers in such Form, as to them shall seem most likely to effect their Safety and Happiness. Prudence, indeed, will dictate that Governments long established should not be changed for light and transient Causes; and accordingly all Experience hath shewn, that Mankind are more disposed to suffer, while Evils are sufferable, than to right themselves by abolishing the Forms to which they are accustomed. But when a long Train of Abuses and Usurpations, pursuing invariably the same Object, evinces a Design to reduce them under absolute Despotism, it is their Right, it is their Duty, to throw off such Government, and to provide new Guards for their future Security. Such has been the patient Sufferance of these Colonies; and such is now the Necessity which constrains them to alter their former Systems of Government. The History of the present King of Great-Britain is a History of repeated Injuries and Usurpations, all having in direct Object the Establishment of an absolute Tyranny over these States. To prove this, let Facts be submitted to a candid World.

HE has refused his Assent to Laws, the most wholesome and necessary for the public Good.

HE has forbidden his Governors to pass Laws of immediate and pressing Importance, unless suspended in their Operation till his Assent should be obtained; and when so suspended, he has utterly neglected to attend to them.

HE has refused to pass other Laws for the Accommodation of large Districts of People, unless those People would relinquish the Right of Representation in the Legislature, a Right inestimable to them, and formidable to Tyrants only.

HE has called together Legislative Bodies at Places unusual, uncomfortable, and distant from the Depository of their public Records, for the sole Purpose of fatiguing them into Compliance with his Measures.

HE has dissolved Representative Houses repeatedly, for opposing with manly Firmness his Invasions on the Rights of the People.

HE has refused for a long Time, after such Dissolutions, to cause others to be elected; whereby the Legislative Powers, incapable of Annihilation, have returned to the People at large for their exercise; the State remaining in the mean time exposed to all the Dangers of Invasion from without, and Convulsions within.

HE has endeavoured to prevent the Population of these States; for that Purpose obstructing the Laws for Naturalization of Foreigners; refusing to pass others to encourage their Migrations hither, and raising the Conditions of new Appropriations of Lands.

HE has obstructed the Administration of Justice, by refusing his Assent to Laws for establishing Judiciary Powers.

HE has made Judges dependent on his Will alone, for the Tenure of their Offices, and the Amount and Payment of their Salaries.

HE has erected a Multitude of new Offices, and sent hither Swarms of Officers to harrass our People, and eat out their Substance.

HE has kept among us, in Times of Peace, Standing Armies, without the consent of our Legislatures.

HE has affected to render the Military independent of and superior to the Civil Power.

HE has combined with others to subject us to a Jurisdiction foreign to our Constitution, and unacknowledged by our Laws; giving his Assent to their Acts of pretended Legislation:

For quartering large Bodies of Armed Troops among us:

For protecting them, by a mock Trial, from Punishment for any Murders which they should commit on the Inhabitants of these States:

For cutting off our Trade with all Parts of the World:

For imposing Taxes on us without our Consent:

For depriving us, in many Cases, of the Benefits of Trial by Jury:

For transporting us beyond Seas to be tried for pretended Offences:

For abolishing the free System of English Laws in a neighbouring Province, establishing therein an arbitrary Government, and enlarging its Boundaries, so as to render it at once an Example and fit Instrument for introducing the same absolute Rule into these Colonies:

For taking away our Charters, abolishing our most valuable Laws, and altering fundamentally the Forms of our Governments:

For suspending our own Legislatures, and declaring themselves invested with Power to legislate for us in all Cases whatsoever.

He has abdicated Government here, by declaring us out of his Protection and waging War against us.

He has plundered our Seas, ravaged our Coasts, burnt our Towns, and destroyed the Lives of our People.

He is, at this Time, transporting large Armies of foreign Mercenaries to compleat the Works of Death, Desolation, and Tyranny, already begun with circumstances of Cruelty and Perfidy, scarcely paralleled in the most barbarous Ages, and totally unworthy the Head of a civilized Nation.

He has constrained our fellow Citizens taken Captive on the high Seas to bear Arms against their Country, to become the Executioners of their Friends and Brethren, or to fall themselves by their Hands.

HE has excited domestic Insurrections amongst us, and has endeavoured to bring on the Inhabitants of our Frontiers, the merciless Indian Savages, whose known Rule of Warfare, is an undistinguished Destruction, of all Ages, Sexes and Conditions.

IN every stage of these Oppressions we have Petitioned for Redress in the most humble Terms: Our repeated Petitions have been answered only by repeated Injury. A Prince, whose Character is thus marked by every act which may define a Tyrant, is unfit to be the Ruler of a free People.

NOR have we been wanting in Attentions to our British Brethren. We have warned them from Time to Time of Attempts by their Legislature to extend an unwarrantable Jurisdiction over us. We have reminded them of the Circumstances of our Emigration and Settlement here. We have appealed to their native Justice and Magnanimity, and we have conjured them by the Ties of our common Kindred to disavow these Usurpations, which, would inevitably interrupt our Connections and Correspondence. They too have been deaf to the Voice of Justice and of Consanguinity. We must, therefore, acquiesce in the Necessity, which denounces our Separation, and hold them, as we hold the rest of Mankind, Enemies in War, in Peace, Friends.

WE, therefore, the Representatives of the UNITED STATES OF AMERICA, in GENERAL CONGRESS, Assembled, appealing to the Supreme Judge of the World for the Rectitude of our Intentions, do, in the Name, and by Authority of the good People of these Colonies, solemnly Publish and Declare, That these United Colonies are, and of Right ought to be, FREE AND INDEPENDENT STATES; that they are absolved from all Allegiance to the British Crown, and that all political Connection between them and the State of Great-Britain, is and ought to be totally dissolved; and that as FREE AND INDEPENDENT STATES, they have full Power to levy War, conclude Peace, contract Alliances, establish Commerce, and to do all other Acts and Things which INDEPENDENT STATES may of right do. And for the support of this Declaration, with a firm Reliance on the Protection of divine Providence, we mutually pledge to each other our Lives, our Fortunes, and our sacred Honor.

THE CONSTITUTION OF
THE UNITED STATES

WE THE People of the United States, in Order to form a more perfect Union, establish Justice, insure domestic Tranquility, provide for the common defence, promote the general Welfare, and secure the Blessings of Liberty to ourselves and our Posterity, do ordain and establish this Constitution for the United States of America.

ARTICLE. I.

Section. 1. All legislative Powers herein granted shall be vested in a Congress of the United States, which shall consist of a Senate and House of Representatives.

Section. 2. The House of Representatives shall be composed of Members chosen every second Year by the People of the several States, and the Electors in each State shall have the Qualifications requisite for Electors of the most numerous Branch of the State Legislature.

No Person shall be a Representative who shall not have attained to the Age of twenty-five Years, and been seven Years a Citizen of the United States, and who shall not, when elected, be an Inhabitant of that State in which he shall be chosen.

[Representatives and direct Taxes shall be apportioned among the several States which may be included within this Union, according to their respective Numbers, which shall be determined by adding to the whole Number of free Persons, including those bound to Service for a Term of Years, and excluding Indians not taxed, three fifths of all other Persons.]* The actual Enumeration shall be made within three Years after the first Meeting of the Congress of the United States, and within every subsequent Term of ten Years, in such Manner as they shall by Law direct. The number of Representatives shall not exceed one for every thirty Thousand, but each State shall have at Least one Representative; and until such enumeration shall be made, the State of New Hampshire shall be entitled to chuse three, Massachusetts eight, Rhode-Island and Providence Plantations one, Connecticut five, New-York six, New Jersey four, Pennsylvania eight, Delaware one, Maryland six, Virginia ten, North Carolina five, South Carolina five, and Georgia three.

When vacancies happen in the Representation from any State, the Executive Authority thereof shall issue Writs of Election to fill such Vacancies.

The House of Representatives shall chuse their Speaker and other Officers; and shall have the sole Power of Impeachment.

Section. 3. The Senate of the United States shall be composed of two Senators from each State, [chosen by the Legislature thereof,]** for six Years; and each Senator shall have one Vote.

Immediately after they shall be assembled in Conse-

*Changed by Section 2 of the Fourteenth Amendment.
**Changed by the Seventeenth Amendment.

quence of the first Election, they shall be divided as equally as may be into three Classes. The Seats of the Senators of the first Class shall be vacated at the Expiration of the second Year, of the second Class at the Expiration of the fourth Year, and of the third Class at the Expiration of the sixth Year, so that one third may be chosen every second Year; [and if Vacancies happen by Resignation, or otherwise, during the Recess of the Legislature of any State, the Executive thereof may make temporary Appointments until the next Meeting of the Legislature, which shall then fill such Vacancies.]*

No Person shall be a Senator who shall not have attained to the Age of thirty Years, and been nine Years a Citizen of the United States, and who shall not, when elected, be an Inhabitant of that State for which he shall be chosen.

The Vice President of the United States shall be President of the Senate, but shall have no Vote, unless they be equally divided.

The Senate shall chuse their other Officers, and also a President pro tempore, in the Absence of the Vice President, or when he shall exercise the Office of President of the United States.

The Senate shall have the sole Power to try all Impeachments. When sitting for that Purpose, they shall be on Oath or Affirmation. When the President of the United States is tried, the Chief Justice shall preside: And no Person shall be convicted without the Concurrence of two thirds of the Members present.

Judgment in Cases of Impeachment shall not extend further than to removal from Office, and disqualification

*Changed by the Seventeenth Amendment.

to hold and enjoy any Office of honor, Trust or Profit under the United States: but the Party convicted shall nevertheless be liable and subject to Indictment, Trial, Judgment and Punishment, according to Law.

Section. 4. The Times, Places and Manner of holding Elections for Senators and Representatives, shall be prescribed in each State by the Legislature thereof; but the Congress may at any time by Law make or alter such Regulations, except as to the Places of chusing Senators.

The Congress shall assemble at least once in every Year, and such Meeting shall be [on the first Monday in December,]* unless they shall by Law appoint a different Day.

Section. 5. Each House shall be the Judge of the Elections, Returns and Qualifications of its own Members, and a Majority of each shall constitute a Quorum to do Business; but a smaller Number may adjourn from day to day, and may be authorized to compel the Attendance of absent Members, in such Manner, and under such Penalties as each House may provide.

Each House may determine the Rules of its Proceedings, punish its Members for disorderly Behaviour, and, with the Concurrence of two thirds, expel a Member.

Each House shall keep a Journal of its Proceedings, and from time to time publish the same, excepting such Parts as may in their Judgment require Secrecy; and the Yeas and Nays of the Members of either House on any question shall, at the Desire of one fifth of those Present, be entered on the Journal.

Neither House, during the Session of Congress, shall, without the Consent of the other, adjourn for more than

*Changed by section 2 of the Twentieth Amendment.

three days, nor to any other Place than that in which the two Houses shall be sitting.

Section. 6. The Senators and Representatives shall receive a Compensation for their Services, to be ascertained by Law, and paid out of the Treasury of the United States. They shall in all Cases, except Treason, Felony and Breach of the Peace, be privileged from Arrest during their Attendance at the Session of their respective Houses, and in going to and returning from the same; and for any Speech or Debate in either House, they shall not be questioned in any other Place.

No Senator or Representative shall, during the Time for which he was elected, be appointed to any civil Office under the Authority of the United States, which shall have been created, or the Emoluments whereof shall have been encreased during such time; and no Person holding any Office under the United States, shall be a Member of either House during his Continuance in Office.

Section. 7. All Bills for raising Revenue shall originate in the House of Representatives; but the Senate may propose or concur with Amendments as on other Bills.

Every Bill which shall have passed the House of Representatives and the Senate, shall, before it becomes a Law, be presented to the President of the United States; If he approve he shall sign it, but if not he shall return it, with his Objections to that House in which it shall have originated, who shall enter the Objections at large on their Journal, and proceed to reconsider it. If after such Reconsideration two thirds of that House shall agree to pass the Bill, it shall be sent, together with the Objections, to the other House, by which it shall likewise be reconsidered, and if approved by two thirds of that House, it shall become a Law. But in all such Cases the

Votes of both Houses shall be determined by yeas and Nays, and the Names of the Persons voting for and against the Bill shall be entered on the Journal of each House respectively. If any Bill shall not be returned by the President within ten Days (Sundays excepted) after it shall have been presented to him, the Same shall be a Law, in like Manner as if he had signed it, unless the Congress by their Adjournment prevent its Return, in which Case it shall not be a Law.

Every Order, Resolution, or Vote to which the Concurrence of the Senate and House of Representatives may be necessary (except on a question of Adjournment) shall be presented to the President of the United States; and before the Same shall take Effect, shall be approved by him, or being disapproved by him, shall be repassed by two thirds of the Senate and House of Representatives, according to the Rules and Limitations prescribed in the Case of a Bill.

Section. 8. The Congress shall have Power To lay and collect Taxes, Duties, Imposts and Excises, to pay the Debts and provide for the common Defence and general Welfare of the United States; but all Duties, Imposts and Excises shall be uniform throughout the United States;

To borrow Money on the credit of the United States;

To regulate Commerce with foreign Nations, and among the several States, and with the Indian Tribes;

To establish an uniform Rule of Naturalization, and uniform Laws on the subject of Bankruptcies throughout the United States;

To coin Money, regulate the Value thereof, and of foreign Coin, and fix the Standard of Weights and Measures;

To provide for the Punishment of counterfeiting the Securities and current Coin of the United States;

To establish Post Offices and post Roads;

To promote the Progress of Science and useful Arts, by securing for limited Times to Authors and Inventors the exclusive Right to their respective Writings and Discoveries;

To constitute Tribunals inferior to the supreme Court;

To definc and punish Piracies and Felonies committed on the high Seas, and Offenses against the Law of Nations;

To declare War, grant Letters of Marque and Reprisal, and make Rules concerning Captures on Land and Water;

To raise and support Armies, but no Appropriation of Money to that Use shall be for a longer Term than two Years;

To provide and maintain a Navy;

To make Rules for the Government and Regulation of the land and naval Forces;

To provide for calling forth the Militia to execute the Laws of the Union, suppress Insurrections and repel Invasions;

To provide for organizing, arming, and disciplining, the Militia, and for governing such Part of them as may be employed in the Service of the United States, reserving to the States respectively, the Appointment of the Officers, and the Authority of training the Militia according to the discipline prescribed by Congress;

To exercise exclusive Legislation in all Cases whatsoever, over such District (not exceeding ten Miles square) as may, by Cession of particular States, and the Acceptance of Congress, become the Seat of the Government of the United States, and to exercise like Authority over all Places purchased by the Consent of the Legislature of the State in which the Same shall be, for the Erection of

Forts, Magazines, Arsenals, dock-Yards and other needful Buildings;—And

To make all Laws which shall be necessary and proper for carrying into Execution the foregoing Powers, and all other Powers vested by this Constitution in the Government of the United States, or in any Department or Officer thereof.

Section. 9. The Migration or Importation of such Persons as any of the States now existing shall think proper to admit, shall not be prohibited by the Congress prior to the Year one thousand eight hundred and eight, but a Tax or duty may be imposed on such Importation, not exceeding ten dollars for each Person.

The Privilege of the Writ of Habeas Corpus shall not be suspended, unless when in Cases of Rebellion or Invasion the public Safety may require it.

No Bill of Attainder or ex post facto Law shall be passed.

No Capitation, or other direct, Tax shall be laid, unless in Proportion to the Census or Enumeration herein before directed to be taken.*

No Tax or Duty shall be laid on Articles exported from any State.

No Preference shall be given by any Regulation of Commerce or Revenue to the Ports of one State over those of another: nor shall Vessels bound to, or from, one State, be obliged to enter, clear, or pay Duties in another.

No Money shall be drawn from the Treasury, but in Consequence of Appropriations made by Law; and a regular Statement and Account of the Receipts and Expenditures of all public Money shall be published from time to time.

---

*See Sixteenth Amendment.

No Title of Nobility shall be granted by the United States: and no Person holding any Office of Profit or Trust under them, shall, without the Consent of the Congress, accept of any present, Emolument, Office, or Title, of any kind whatever, from any King, Prince, or foreign State.

Section. 10. No State shall enter into any Treaty, Alliance, or Confederation; grant Letters of Marque and Reprisal; coin Money; emit Bills of Credit; make any Thing but gold and silver Coin a Tender in Payment of Debts; pass any Bill of Attainder, ex post facto Law, or Law impairing the Obligation of Contracts, or grant any Title of Nobility.

No State shall, without the Consent of the Congress, lay any Imposts or Duties on Imports or Exports, except what may be absolutely necessary for executing it's inspection Laws: and the net Produce of all Duties and Imposts, laid by any State on Imports or Exports, shall be for the Use of the Treasury of the United States; and all such Laws shall be subject to the Revision and Controul of the Congress.

No State shall, without the Consent of Congress, lay any Duty of Tonnage, keep Troops, or Ships of War in time of Peace, enter into any Agreement or Compact with another State, or with a foreign Power, or engage in War, unless actually invaded, or in such imminent Danger as will not admit of delay.

ARTICLE. II.

Section. 1. The executive Power shall be vested in a President of the United States of America. He shall hold his Office during the Term of four Years, and, together with the Vice President, chosen for the same Term, be elected, as follows

Each State shall appoint, in such Manner as the Legislature thereof may direct, a Number of Electors, equal to the whole Number of Senators and Representatives to which the State may be entitled in the Congress: but no Senator or Representative, or Person holding an Office of Trust or Profit under the United States, shall be appointed an Elector.

[The Electors shall meet in their respective States, and vote by Ballot for two Persons, of whom one at least shall not be an Inhabitant of the same State with themselves. And they shall make a List of all the Persons voted for, and of the Number of Votes for each; which List they shall sign and certify, and transmit sealed to the Seat of the Government of the United States, directed to the President of the Senate. The President of the Senate shall, in the Presence of the Senate and House of Representatives, open all the Certificates, and the Votes shall then be counted. The Person having the greatest Number of Votes shall be the President, if such Number be a Majority of the whole Number of Electors appointed; and if there be more than one who have such Majority, and have an equal Number of Votes, then the House of Representatives shall immediately chuse by Ballot one of them for President; and if no Person have a Majority, then from the five highest on the List the said House shall in like Manner chuse the President. But in chusing the President, the Votes shall be taken by States, the Representation from each State having one Vote; A quorum for this Purpose shall consist of a Member or Members from two thirds of the States, and a Majority of all the States shall be necessary to a Choice. In every

Case, after the Choice of the President, the Person having the greatest Number of Votes of the Electors shall be the Vice President. But if there should remain two or more who have equal Votes, the Senate shall chuse from them by Ballot the Vice President.]*

The Congress may determine the Time of chusing the Electors, and the Day on which they shall give their Votes; which Day shall be the same throughout the United States.

No Person except a natural born Citizen, or a Citizen of the United States, at the time of the Adoption of this Constitution, shall be eligible to the Office of President; neither shall any person be eligible to that Office who shall not have attained to the Age of thirty five Years, and been fourteen Years a Resident within the United States.

[In Case of the Removal of the President from Office, or of his Death, Resignation, or Inability to discharge the Powers and Duties of the said Office, the Same shall devolve on the Vice President, and the Congress may by Law provide for the Case of Removal, Death, Resignation or Inability, both of the President and Vice President, declaring what Officer shall then act as President, and such Officer shall act accordingly, until the Disability be removed, or a President shall be elected.]**

The President shall, at stated Times, receive for his Services, a Compensation, which shall neither be increased nor diminished during the Period for which he shall have been elected, and he shall not receive within that Period any other Emolument from the United States, or any of them.

*Changed by the Twelfth Amendment.
**Changed by the Twenty-Fifth Amendment.

Before he enter on the Execution of his Office, he shall take the following Oath or Affirmation:—"I do solemnly swear (or affirm) that I will faithfully execute the Office of President of the United States, and will to the best of my Ability, preserve, protect and defend the Constitution of the United States."

Section. 2. The President shall be Commander in Chief of the Army and Navy of the United States, and of the Militia of the several States, when called into the actual Service of the United States; he may require the Opinion, in writing, of the principal Officer in each of the executive Departments, upon any Subject relating to the Duties of their respective Offices, and he shall have Power to grant Reprieves and Pardons for Offenses against the United States, except in Cases of Impeachment.

He shall have Power; by and with the Advice and Consent of the Senate, to make Treaties, provided two thirds of the Senators present concur; and he shall nominate, and by and with the Advice and Consent of the Senate, shall appoint Ambassadors, other public Ministers and Consuls, Judges of the supreme Court, and all other Officers of the United States, whose Appointments are not herein otherwise provided for, and which shall be established by Law: but the Congress may by Law vest the Appointment of such inferior Officers, as they think proper, in the President alone, in the Courts of Law, or in the Heads of Departments.

The President shall have Power to fill up all Vacancies that may happen during the Recess of the Senate, by granting Commissions which shall expire at the End of their next Session.

Section. 3. He shall from time to time give to the Congress Information of the State of the Union, and recommend to their Consideration such Measures as he shall judge necessary and expedient; he may, on extraordinary Occasions, convene both Houses, or either of them, and in Case of Disagreement between them, with Respect to the Time of Adjournment, he may adjourn them to such Time as he shall think proper; he shall receive Ambassadors and other public Ministers; he shall take Care that the Laws be faithfully executed, and shall Commission all the Officers of the United States.

Section. 4. The President, Vice President and all civil Officers of the United States, shall be removed from Office on Impeachment for, and Conviction of, Treason, Bribery, or other high Crimes and Misdemeanors.

ARTICLE. III.

Section. 1. The judicial Power of the United States, shall be vested in one supreme Court, and in such inferior Courts as the Congress may from time to time ordain and establish. The Judges, both of the supreme and inferior Courts, shall hold their Offices during good Behaviour, and shall, at stated Times, receive for their Services, a Compensation, which shall not be diminished during their Continuance in Office.

Section. 2. The judicial Power shall extend to all Cases, in Law and Equity, arising under this Constitution, the Laws of the United States, and Treaties made, or which shall be made, under their Authority;—to all Cases affecting Ambassadors, other public Ministers and Consuls;—to all Cases of admiralty and maritime Jurisdiction;—to Controversies to which the United States shall be a Party;—to Controversies between two or more States;—[between a State and Citizens of another

State;—] between Citizens of different States,—between Citizens of the same State claiming Lands under Grants of different States, [and between a State, or the Citizens thereof, and foreign States, Citizens or Subjects.]*

In all Cases affecting Ambassadors, other public Ministers and Consuls, and those in which a State shall be Party, the supreme Court shall have original Jurisdiction. In all the other Cases before mentioned, the supreme Court shall have appellate Jurisdiction, both as to Law and Fact, with such Exceptions, and under such Regulations as the Congress shall make.

The Trial of all Crimes, except in Cases of Impeachment; shall be by Jury; and such Trial shall be held in the State where the said Crimes shall have been committed; but when not committed within any State, the Trial shall be at such Place or Places as the Congress may by Law have directed.

Section. 3. Treason against the United States, shall consist only in levying War against them, or in adhering to their Enemies, giving them Aid and Comfort. No Person shall be convicted of Treason unless on the Testimony of two Witnesses to the same overt Act, or on Confession in open Court.

The Congress shall have Power to declare the Punishment of Treason, but no Attainder of Treason shall work Corruption of Blood, or Forfeiture except during the Life of the Person attainted.

ARTICLE. IV.

Section. 1. Full Faith and Credit shall be given in each State to the public Acts, Records, and judicial Proceedings

*Changed by the Eleventh Amendment.

of every other State; And the Congress may by general Laws prescribe the Manner in which such Acts, Records and Proceedings shall be proved, and the Effect thereof.

Section. 2. The Citizens of each State shall be entitled to all Privileges and Immunities of Citizens in the several States.

A Person charged in any State with Treason, Felony, or other Crime, who shall flee from Justice, and be found in another State, shall on Demand of the executive Authority of the State from which he fled, be delivered up, to be removed to the State having Jurisdiction of the Crime.

[No Person held to Service or Labour in one State, under the Laws thereof, escaping into another, shall, in Consequence of any Law or Regulation therein, be discharged from such Service or Labour, but shall be delivered up on Claim of the Party to whom such Service or Labour may be due.]*

Section. 3. New States may be admitted by the Congress into this Union; but no new State shall be formed or erected within the Jurisdiction of any other State; nor any State be formed by the Junction of two or more States, or Parts of States, without the Consent of the Legislatures of the States concerned as well as of the Congress.

The Congress shall have Power to dispose of and make all needful Rules and Regulations respecting the Territory or other Property belonging to the United States; and nothing in this Constitution shall be so construed as to Prejudice any Claims of the United States, or of any particular State.

Section. 4. The United States shall guarantee to every

---

*Changed by the Thirteenth Amendment.

State in this Union a Republican Form of Government, and shall protect each of them against Invasion; and on Application of the Legislature, or of the Executive (when the Legislature cannot be convened) against domestic Violence.

ARTICLE. V.

The Congress, whenever two thirds of both Houses shall deem it necessary, shall propose Amendments to this Constitution, or, on the Application of the Legislatures of two thirds of the several States, shall call a Convention for proposing Amendments, which, in either Case, shall be valid to all Intents and Purposes, as Part of this Constitution, when ratified by the Legislatures of three fourths of the several States, or by Conventions in three fourths thereof, as the one or the other Mode of Ratification may be proposed by the Congress; Provided that no Amendment which may be made prior to the Year One thousand eight hundred and eight shall in any Manner affect the first and fourth Clauses in the Ninth Section of the first Article; and that no State, without its Consent, shall be deprived of its equal Suffrage in the Senate.

ARTICLE. VI.

All Debts contracted and Engagements entered into, before the Adoption of this Constitution, shall be as valid against the United States under this Constitution, as under the Confederation.

This Constitution, and the Laws of the United States which shall be made in Pursuance thereof; and all Treaties made, or which shall be made, under the Authority of the United States, shall be the supreme Law of the Land; and the Judges in every State shall be bound thereby, any Thing in the Constitution or Laws of any State to the Contrary notwithstanding.

The Senators and Representatives before mentioned, and the Members of the several State Legislatures, and all executive and judicial Officers, both of the United States and of the several States, shall be bound by Oath or Affirmation, to support this Constitution; but no religious Test shall ever be required as a Qualification to any Office or public Trust under the United States.

ARTICLE. VII.

The Ratification of the Conventions of nine States, shall be sufficient for the Establishment of this Constitution between the States so ratifying the Same.

Done in Convention by the Unanimous Consent of the States present the Seventeenth Day of September in the Year of our Lord one thousand seven hundred and Eighty seven and of the Independence of the United States of America the Twelfth In Witness whereof We have hereunto subscribed our Names,

G°. Washington—Presid!
and deputy from Virginia

Delaware	*Geo: Read*
	Gunning Bedford jun
	John Dickinson
	Richard Bassett
	Jaco: Broom
Maryland	*James McHenry*
	Dan of St. Thos. Jenifer
	Danl. Carroll

Virginia	*John Blair*
	James Madison Jr.
North Carolina	*Wm. Blount*
	Richd. Dobbs Spaight
	Hu Williamson
South Carolina	*J. Rutledge*
	Charles Cotesworth
	* Pinckney*
	Charles Pinckney
	Pierce Butler
Georgia	*William Few*
	Abr Baldwin
New Hampshire	*John Langdon*
	Nicholas Gilman
Massachusetts	*Nathaniel Gorham*
	Rufus King
Connecticut	*Wm. Saml. Johnson*
	Roger Sherman
New York	*Alexander Hamilton*
New Jersey	*Wil: Livingston*
	David Brearley
	Wm. Paterson
	Jona: Dayton
Pennsylvania	*B. Franklin*
	Thomas Mifflin
	Robt. Morris
	Geo. Clymer
	Thos. FitzSimons
	Jared Ingersoll
	James Wilson
	Gouv Morris

Attest William Jackson Secretary

THE AMENDMENTS TO THE CONSTITUTION OF THE UNITED STATES OF AMERICA

AMENDMENT I.*

CONGRESS SHALL make no law respecting an establishment of religion, or prohibiting the free exercise thereof; or abridging the freedom of speech, or of the press, or the right of the people peaceably to assemble, and to petition the Government for a redress of grievances.

AMENDMENT II.

A well regulated Militia, being necessary to the security of a free State, the right of the people to keep and bear Arms, shall not be infringed.

AMENDMENT III.

No Soldier shall, in time of peace be quartered in any house, without the consent of the Owner, nor in time of war, but in a manner to be prescribed by law.

*The first ten Amendments (Bill of Rights) were ratified effective December 15, 1791.

AMENDMENT IV.

The right of the people to be secure in their persons, houses, papers, and effects, against unreasonable searches and seizures, shall not be violated, and no Warrants shall issue, but upon probable cause, supported by Oath or affirmation, and particularly describing the place to be searched, and the persons or things to be seized.

AMENDMENT V.

No person shall be held to answer for a capital, or otherwise infamous crime, unless on a presentment or indictment of a Grand Jury, except in cases arising in the land or naval forces, or in the Militia, when in actual service in time of War or public danger; nor shall any person be subject for the same offence to be twice put in jeopardy of life or limb, nor shall be compelled in any criminal case to be a witness against himself, nor be deprived of life, liberty, or property, without due process of law; nor shall private property be taken for public use without just compensation.

AMENDMENT VI.

In all criminal prosecutions, the accused shall enjoy the right to a speedy and public trial, by an impartial jury of the State and district wherein the crime shall have been committed; which district shall have been previously ascertained by law, and to be informed of the nature and cause of the accusation; to be confronted with the witnesses against him; to have compulsory process for obtaining witnesses in his favor, and to have the assistance of counsel for his defence.

AMENDMENT VII.

In Suits at common law, where the value in controversy shall exceed twenty dollars, the right of trial by jury shall be preserved, and no fact tried by a jury shall be otherwise re-examined in any Court of the United States, than according to the rules of the common law.

AMENDMENT VIII.

Excessive bail shall not be required, nor excessive fines imposed, nor cruel and unusual punishments inflicted.

AMENDMENT IX.

The enumeration in the Constitution of certain rights shall not be construed to deny or disparage others retained by the people.

AMENDMENT X.

The powers not delegated to the United States by the Constitution, nor prohibited by it to the States, are reserved to the States respectively, or to the people.

AMENDMENT XI.*

The Judicial power of the United States shall not be construed to extend to any suit in law or equity, commenced or prosecuted against one of the United States by Citizens

*The Eleventh Amendment was ratified February 7, 1795.

of another State, or by Citizens or Subjects of any Foreign State.

AMENDMENT XII.*

The Electors shall meet in their respective states, and vote by ballot for President and Vice-President, one of whom, at least, shall not be an inhabitant of the same state with themselves; they shall name in their ballots the person voted for as President, and in distinct ballots the person voted for as Vice-President, and they shall make distinct lists of all persons voted for as President, and of all persons voted for as Vice-President, and of the number of votes for each, which lists they shall sign and certify, and transmit sealed to the seat of the government of the United States, directed to the President of the Senate;—The President of the Senate shall, in the presence of the Senate and House of Representatives, open all the certificates and the votes shall then be counted;—The person having the greatest number of votes for President, shall be the President, if such number be a majority of the whole number of Electors appointed; and if no person have such majority, then from the persons having the highest numbers not exceeding three on the list of those voted for as President, the House of Representatives shall choose immediately, by ballot, the President. But in choosing the President, the votes shall be taken by states, the representation from each state having one vote; a quorum for this purpose shall consist of a member or members from two-thirds of the states, and a majority of all the states shall be necessary to a choice. [And if the House of

*The Twelfth Amendment was ratified June 15, 1804.

Representatives shall not choose a President whenever the right of choice shall devolve upon them, before the fourth day of March next following, then the Vice-President shall act as President, as in the case of the death or other constitutional disability of the President—]* The person having the greatest number of votes as Vice-President, shall be the Vice-President, if such number be a majority of the whole number of Electors appointed, and if no person have a majority, then from the two highest numbers on the list, the Senate shall choose the Vice-President; a quorum for the purpose shall consist of two-thirds of the whole number of Senators, and a majority of the whole number shall be necessary to a choice. But no person constitutionally ineligible to the office of President shall be eligible to that of Vice-President of the United States.

AMENDMENT XIII.**

Section 1. Neither slavery nor involuntary servitude, except as a punishment for crime whereof the party shall have been duly convicted, shall exist within the United States, or any place subject to their jurisdiction.

Section 2. Congress shall have power to enforce this article by appropriate legislation.

AMENDMENT XIV.***

Section 1. All persons born or naturalized in the United States and subject to the jurisdiction thereof, are citizens

*Superseded by section 3 of the Twentieth Amendment.

**The Thirteenth Amendment was ratified December 6, 1865.

***The Fourteenth Amendment was ratified July 9, 1868.

of the United States and of the State wherein they reside. No State shall make or enforce any law which shall abridge the privileges or immunities of citizens of the United States; nor shall any State deprive any person of life, liberty, or property, without due process of law; nor deny to any person within its jurisdiction the equal protection of the laws.

Section 2. Representatives shall be apportioned among the several States according to their respective numbers, counting the whole number of persons in each State, excluding Indians not taxed. But when the right to vote at any election for the choice of electors for President and Vice President of the United States, Representatives in Congress, the Executive and Judicial officers of a State, or the members of the Legislature thereof, is denied to any of the male inhabitants of such State, being twenty-one years of age, and citizens of the United States, or in any way abridged, except for participation in rebellion, or other crime, the basis of representation therein shall be reduced in the proportion which the number of such male citizens shall bear to the whole number of male citizens twenty-one years of age in such State.

Section 3. No person shall be a Senator or Representative in Congress, or elector of President and Vice President, or hold any office, civil or military, under the United States, or under any State, who, having previously taken an oath, as a member of Congress, or as an officer of the United States, or as a member of any State legislature, or as an executive or judicial officer of any State, to support the Constitution of the United States, shall have engaged in insurrection or rebellion against the same, or given aid or comfort to the enemies thereof. But Congress may by a vote of two-thirds of each House, remove such disability.

Section 4. The validity of the public debt of the United States, authorized by law, including debts incurred for payment of pensions and bounties for services in suppressing insurrection or rebellion, shall not be questioned. But neither the United States nor any State shall assume or pay any debt or obligation incurred in aid of insurrection or rebellion against the United States, or any claim for the loss or emancipation of any slave; but all such debts, obligations and claims shall be held illegal and void.

Section 5. The Congress shall have power to enforce, by appropriate legislation, the provisions of this article.

AMENDMENT XV.*

Section 1. The right of citizens of the United States to vote shall not be denied or abridged by the United States or by any State on account of race, color, or previous condition of servitude.

Section 2. The Congress shall have power to enforce this article by appropriate legislation.

AMENDMENT XVI.**

The Congress shall have power to lay and collect taxes on incomes, from whatever source derived, without apportionment among the several States, and without regard to any census or enumeration.

*The Fifteenth Amendment was ratified February 3, 1870.
**The Sixteenth Amendment was ratified February 3, 1913.

AMENDMENT XVII.*

The Senate of the United States shall be composed of two Senators from each State, elected by the people thereof, for six years; and each Senator shall have one vote. The electors in each State shall have the qualifications requisite for electors of the most numerous branch of the State legislatures.

When vacancies happen in the representation of any State in the Senate, the executive authority of such State shall issue writs of election to fill such vacancies: *Provided,* That the legislature of any State may empower the executive thereof to make temporary appointments until the people fill the vacancies by election as the legislature may direct.

This amendment shall not be so construed as to affect the election or term of any Senator chosen before it becomes valid as part of the Constitution.

AMENDMENT XVIII.**

[Section 1. After one year from the ratification of this article the manufacture, sale, or transportation of intoxicating liquors within, the importation thereof into, or the exportation thereof from the United States and all territory subject to the jurisdiction thereof for beverage purposes is hereby prohibited.

Section 2. The Congress and the several States shall have concurrent power to enforce this article by appropriate legislation.

*The Seventeenth Amendment was ratified April 8, 1913.

**The Eighteenth Amendment was ratified January 16, 1919. It was repealed by the Twenty-First Amendment, December 5, 1933.

Section 3. This article shall be inoperative unless it shall have been ratified as an amendment to the Constitution by the legislatures of the several States, as provided in the Constitution, within seven years from the date of the submission hereof to the States by the Congress.]

AMENDMENT XIX.*

The right of citizens of the United States to vote shall not be denied or abridged by the United States or by any State on account of sex.

Congress shall have power to enforce this article by appropriate legislation.

AMENDMENT XX.**

Section 1. The terms of the President and Vice President shall end at noon on the 20th day of January, and the terms of Senators and Representatives at noon on the 3d day of January, of the years in which such terms would have ended if this article had not been ratified; and the terms of their successors shall then begin.

Section 2. The Congress shall assemble at least once in every year, and such meeting shall begin at noon on the 3d day of January, unless they shall by law appoint a different day.

Section 3. If, at the time fixed for the beginning of the term of the President, the President elect shall have died, the Vice President elect shall become President. If a President shall not have been chosen before the time fixed

*The Nineteenth Amendment was ratified August 18, 1920.

**The Twentieth Amendment was ratified January 23, 1933.

for the beginning of his term, or if the President elect shall have failed to qualify, then the Vice President elect shall act as President until a President shall have qualified; and the Congress may by law provide for the case wherein neither a President elect nor a Vice President elect shall have qualified, declaring who shall then act as President, or the manner in which one who is to act shall be selected, and such person shall act accordingly until a President or Vice President shall have qualified.

Section 4. The Congress may by law provide for the case of the death of any of the persons from whom the House of Representatives may choose a President whenever the right of choice shall have devolved upon them, and for the case of the death of any of the persons from whom the Senate may choose a Vice President whenever the right of choice shall have devolved upon them.

Section 5. Sections 1 and 2 shall take effect on the 15th day of October following the ratification of this article.

Section 6. This article shall be inoperative unless it shall have been ratified as an amendment to the Constitution by the legislatures of three-fourths of the several States within seven years from the date of its submission.

AMENDMENT XXI.*

Section 1. The eighteenth article of amendment to the Constitution of the United States is hereby repealed.

Section 2. The transportation or importation into any State, Territory, or possession of the United States for delivery or use therein of intoxicating liquors, in violation of the laws thereof, is hereby prohibited.

*The Twenty-first Amendment was ratified December 5, 1933.

Section 3. This article shall be inoperative unless it shall have been ratified as an amendment to the Constitution by conventions in the several States, as provided in the Constitution, within seven years from the date of the submission hereof to the States by the Congress.

AMENDMENT XXII.*

Section 1. No person shall be elected to the office of the President more than twice, and no person who has held the office of President, or acted as President, for more than two years of a term to which some other person was elected President shall be elected to the office of the President more than once. But this Article shall not apply to any person holding the office of President when this Article was proposed by the Congress, and shall not prevent any person who may be holding the office of President, or acting as President, during the term within which this Article becomes operative from holding the office of President or acting as President during the remainder of such term.

Section 2. This article shall be inoperative unless it shall have been ratified as an amendment to the Constitution by the legislatures of three-fourths of the several States within seven years from the date of its submission to the States by the Congress.

AMENDMENT XXIII.**

Section 1. The District constituting the seat of Government of the United States shall appoint in such manner as the Congress may direct:

*The Twenty-second Amendment was ratified February 27, 1951.

**The Twenty-third Amendment was ratified March 29, 1961.

A number of electors of President and Vice President equal to the whole number of Senators and Representatives in Congress to which the District would be entitled if it were a State, but in no event more than the least populous State; they shall be in addition to those appointed by the States, but they shall be considered, for the purposes of the election of President and Vice President, to be electors appointed by a State; and they shall meet in the District and perform such duties as provided by the twelfth article of amendment.

Section 2. The Congress shall have power to enforce this article by appropriate legislation.

AMENDMENT XXIV.*

Section 1. The right of citizens of the United States to vote in any primary or other election for President or Vice President, for electors for President or Vice President, or for Senator or Representative in Congress, shall not be denied or abridged by the United States or any State by reason of failure to pay any poll tax or other tax.

Section 2. The Congress shall have power to enforce this article by appropriate legislation.

AMENDMENT XXV.**

Section 1. In case of the removal of the President from office or of his death or resignation, the Vice President shall become President.

Section 2. Whenever there is a vacancy in the office of the Vice President, the President shall nominate a Vice

---

*The Twenty-fourth Amendment was ratified January 23, 1964.

**The Twenty-fifth Amendment was ratified February 10, 1967.

President who shall take office upon confirmation by a majority vote of both Houses of Congress.

Section 3. Whenever the President transmits to the President pro tempore of the Senate and the Speaker of the House of Representatives his written declaration that he is unable to discharge the powers and duties of his office, and until he transmits to them a written declaration to the contrary, such powers and duties shall be discharged by the Vice President as Acting President.

Section 4. Whenever the Vice President and a majority of either the principal officers of the executive departments or of such other body as Congress may by law provide, transmit to the President pro tempore of the Senate and the Speaker of the House of Representatives their written declaration that the President is unable to discharge the powers and duties of his office, the Vice President shall immediately assume the powers and duties of the office as Acting President.

Thereafter, when the President transmits to the President pro tempore of the Senate and the Speaker of the House of Representatives his written declaration that no inability exists, he shall resume the powers and duties of his office unless the Vice President and a majority of either the principal officers of the executive department or of such other body as Congress may by law provide, transmit within four days to the President pro tempore of the Senate and the Speaker of the House of Representatives their written declaration that the President is unable to discharge the powers and duties of his office. Thereupon Congress shall decide the issue, assembling within forty-eight hours for that purpose if not in session. If the Congress, within twenty-one days after receipt of the latter written declaration, or, if Congress is not in session, within twenty-one days after

Congress is required to assemble, determines by two-thirds vote of both Houses that the President is unable to discharge the powers and duties of his office, the Vice President shall continue to discharge the same as Acting President; otherwise, the President shall resume the powers and duties of his office.

AMENDMENT XXVI.*

Section 1. The right of citizens of the United States, who are eighteen years of age or older, to vote shall not be denied or abridged by the United States or by any State on account of age.

Section 2. The Congress shall have power to enforce this article by appropriate legislation.

AMENDMENT XXVII.**

No law, varying the compensation for the services of the Senators and Representatives, shall take effect, until an election of Representatives shall have intervened.

---

*The Twenty-sixth Amendment was ratified July 1, 1971.

**Congress submitted the text of the Twenty-seventh Amendment to the states as part of the proposed Bill of Rights on September 25, 1789. The Amendment was not ratified together with the first ten Amendments, which became effective on December 15, 1791. The Twenty-seventh Amendment was ratified on May 7, 1992, by the vote of Michigan.

DATES TO REMEMBER

May 25, 1787: The Constitutional Convention opens with a quorum of seven states in Philadelphia to discuss revising the Articles of Confederation. Eventually all states but Rhode Island are represented.

Sept. 17, 1787: All 12 state delegations approve the Constitution, 39 delegates sign it of the 42 present, and the Convention formally adjourns.

June 21, 1788: The Constitution becomes effective for the ratifying states when New Hampshire is the ninth state to ratify it.

March 4, 1789: The first Congress under the Constitution convenes in New York City.

April 30, 1789: George Washington is inaugurated as the first President of the United States.

June 8, 1789: James Madison introduces proposed Bill of Rights in the House of Representatives.

Sept. 24, 1789: Congress establishes a Supreme Court, 13 district courts, three ad hoc circuit courts, and the position of Attorney General.

Sept. 25, 1789: Congress approves 12 amendments and sends them to the states for ratification.

Feb. 2, 1790: Supreme Court convenes for the first time after an unsuccessful attempt February 1.

Dec. 15, 1791: Virginia ratifies the Bill of Rights, and 10 of the 12 proposed amendments become part of the U.S. Constitution.

INDEX TO CONSTITUTION
AND AMENDMENTS

94

96

ASK YOUR BOOKSELLER
FOR THESE BANTAM CLASSICS

SILAS MARNER, George Eliot, 978-0-553-21229-7

SELECTED ESSAYS, LECTURES, AND POEMS, Ralph Waldo Emerson,
978-0-553-21388-1

TEN PLAYS BY EURIPIDES, Euripides, 978-0-553-21363-8

APRIL MORNING, Howard Fast, 978-0-553-27322-9

MADAME BOVARY, Gustave Flaubert, 978-0-553-21341-6

HOWARDS END, E. M. Forster, 978-0-553-21208-2

A ROOM WITH A VIEW, E. M. Forster, 978-0-553-21323-2

THE DIARY OF A YOUNG GIRL, Anne Frank, 978-0-553-57712-9

ANNE FRANK'S TALES FROM THE SECRET ANNEX, Anne Frank,
978-0-553-58638-1

THE AUTOBIOGRAPHY AND OTHER WRITINGS, Benjamin Franklin,
978-0-553-21075-0

THE YELLOW WALLPAPER AND OTHER WRITINGS, Charlotte Perkins Gilman,
978-0-553-21375-1

FAUST: FIRST PART, Johann Wolfgang von Goethe, 978-0-553-21348-5

THE WIND IN THE WILLOWS, Kenneth Grahame, 978-0-553-21368-3

THE COMPLETE FAIRY TALES OF THE BROTHERS GRIMM,
translated by Jack Zipes, 978-0-553-38216-7

ROOTS, Alex Haley, 978-0-440-17464-6

FAR FROM THE MADDING CROWD, Thomas Hardy, 978-0-553-21331-7

JUDE THE OBSCURE, Thomas Hardy, 978-0-553-21191-7

THE MAYOR OF CASTERBRIDGE, Thomas Hardy, 978-0-553-21024-8

THE RETURN OF THE NATIVE, Thomas Hardy, 978-0-553-21269-3

TESS OF THE D'URBERVILLES, Thomas Hardy, 978-0-553-21168-9

THE HOUSE OF THE SEVEN GABLES, Nathaniel Hawthorne,
978-0-553-21270-9

THE SCARLET LETTER, Nathaniel Hawthorne, 978-0-553-21009-5

THE FAIRY TALES OF HERMANN HESSE, Hermann Hesse, 978-0-553-37776-7

SIDDHARTHA, Hermann Hesse, 978-0-553-20884-9

THE ODYSSEY OF HOMER, Homer, 978-0-553-21399-7

THE HUNCHBACK OF NOTRE DAME, Victor Hugo, 978-0-553-21370-6

FOUR GREAT PLAYS: A DOLL'S HOUSE, GHOSTS, AN ENEMY OF THE PEOPLE,
and THE WILD DUCK, Henrik Ibsen, 978-0-553-21280-8

THE PORTRAIT OF A LADY, Henry James, 978-0-553-21127-6

THE TURN OF THE SCREW AND OTHER SHORT FICTION, Henry James,
978-0-553-21059-0

A COUNTRY DOCTOR, Sarah Orne Jewett, 978-0-553-21498-7

DUBLINERS, James Joyce, 978-0-553-21380-5

A PORTRAIT OF THE ARTIST AS A YOUNG MAN, James Joyce,
978-0-553-21404-8

THE HOUSE OF MIRTH, Edith Wharton, 978-0-553-21320-1

SUMMER, Edith Wharton, 978-0-553-21422-2

LEAVES OF GRASS, Walt Whitman, 978-0-553-21116-0

THE PICTURE OF DORIAN GRAY AND OTHER WRITINGS, Oscar Wilde,
    978-0-553-21254-9

THE SWISS FAMILY ROBINSON, Johann David Wyss, 978-0-553-21403-1

EARLY AFRICAN-AMERICAN CLASSICS, edited by Anthony Appiah,
    978-0-553-21379-9

FIFTY GREAT SHORT STORIES, edited by Milton Crane,
    978-0-553-27745-6

FIFTY GREAT AMERICAN SHORT STORIES, edited by Milton Crane,
    978-0-553-27294-9

SHORT SHORTS, edited by Irving Howe, 978-0-553-27440-0

GREAT AMERICAN SHORT STORIES, edited by Wallace & Mary Stegner,
    978-0-440-33060-8

AMERICAN SHORT STORY MASTERPIECES, edited by Raymond Carver &
    Tom Jenks, 978-0-440-20423-7

SHORT STORY MASTERPIECES, edited by Robert Penn Warren,
    978-0-440-37864-8

THE VOICE THAT IS GREAT WITHIN US, edited by Hayden Carruth,
    978-0-553-26263-6

THE BLACK POETS, edited by Dudley Randal, 978-0-553-27563-6

THREE CENTURIES OF AMERICAN POETRY, edited by Allen Mandelbaum,
    (Trade) 978-0-553-37518-3, (Hardcover) 978-0-553-10250-5